THE WESTWARD MOVEMENT OF THE COTTON ECONOMY 1840-1860

Perceived Interests and Economic Realities

Susan Previant Lee

ARNO PRESS

A New York Times Company

New York / 1977

Editorial Supervision: LUCILLE MAIORCA

————⊸∞⊶————

First publication in book form, Arno Press, 1977

DISSERTATIONS IN AMERICAN ECONOMIC HISTORY
ISBN for complete set: 0-405-09900-2
See last pages of this volume for titles.

Manufactured in the United States of America

————⊸∞⊶————

Library of Congress Cataloging in Publication Data

Lee, Susan.
    The westward movement of the cotton economy, 1840-
1860.

    (Dissertations in American economic history)
    Originally presented as the author's thesis, Columbia,
1975.
    Bibliography: p.
    1. Cotton trade--United States--History. 2. Slavery
in the United States--Economic aspects. 3. Southern
States--Economic conditions. 4. United States--Economic
conditions--To 1865. I. Title. II. Series.
HD9075.3.L44   1977   338.1'7'3510973   76-39832
ISBN 0-405-09912-6

THE WESTWARD MOVEMENT OF THE COTTON
ECONOMY, 1840-1860: PERCEIVED INTERESTS
AND ECONOMIC REALITIES

Susan Previant Lee

Submitted in partial fulfillment of
the requirements for the degree of
Doctor of Philosophy in the Faculty
of Political Science

Columbia University

1975

Acknowledgements

I would like to thank my sponsor, Stuart Bruchey, for
his invaluable assistance. I am grateful also to Peter
Passell and Donald Dewey for their skillful guidance, Deborah
Duff Milenkovitch and Richard B. Morris for providing the
incentive to finish, and Sheila Toomey for correcting my
Shakespeare.

TABLE OF CONTENTS

THE WESTWARD MOVEMENT OF THE COTTON
ECONOMY, 1840-1860: PERCEIVED INTERESTS
AND ECONOMIC REALITIES

CHAPTER I

THE SLAVE ECONOMY: OLD VIEWS AND NEW

The study of history has its own history: from its beginnings as epic and moral tales, to its step toward the fact of documents and records, to its recent advance toward computer centers. History as a social study has begun to give way to history as a social science. Central to this new phase of history, known as quantification, is the use of statistics.

Statistics make possible a considerable refinement in what can be said about the past. That which has been fragmentary or even inaccessible can be rendered useful or reconstructed. For this, statistics has two methods. The first is descriptive -- we can summarize information in a way which makes it more usable, or organize it so that comparisons are possible. The second method is inductive -- we can generalize about a whole population on the basis of just a part of that population.

The use of statistics, theoretical models and hypotheses, all of which are often lumped together under the title of quantification or quanto-history, characterizes what has come to be known as the "new economic history" and the "new political history." The more advanced of the two, in method and technique, is the new economic history. Here, as Stuart Bruchey has pointed out, the rigor of economics, which has sought to transfer the power of the natural sciences into the social sciences, is brought to bear on history.[1] New economic historians, armed with economic theory and statistical analysis, have begun to examine important questions in American history -- from the colonial years through the New Deal.

The antebellum slave economy has come under a great deal of scrutiny by these new historians. Much of this examination has taken the form of profitability studies. The relevance of these studies has been argued by Gavin Wright who discerned several distinct motives for looking into the profitability of slavery: to learn whether slavery would have disappeared for economic reasons without a Civil War; to learn whether slaveowners were "economic men" or whether slaveowning was motivated by other considerations; to understand better the causes of the Civil War, particularly the southern insistence on acquiring new territory and in seceeding from the Union.[2]

But before we can judge the impact that the new economic history has had on our understanding of the economics of slavery, it is necessary and worthwhile to review briefly the old debates. The course of the old economic

---

[1] Stuart Bruchey, The Roots of American Economic Growth (New York, 1968), xv.

[2] Gavin Wright, "New and Old Views of Slavery," Journal of Economic History, xxxiii (June, 1973) 458-459.

historiography reflects the more general outlines of Civil War historiography.[3] Writing in the heat of the Civil War, British economist John Elliot Cairnes echoed the contemporary anti-southern view of the South as a vast slave power conspiracy. His lesson was a moral one, his tone polemic. Slavery, he said, generated an economic system that became the basis of a society populated by an arrogant aristocracy with an inevitable appetite for expansion.

Cairnes felt that originally slavery was economically justified. "*Due to conditions of soil and climate, cultivation by slaves may for a time yield a larger net revenue than cultivation by certain forms of free labor.*"[4] However, that profitability was quickly lost so that virtually the only reason for maintaining slavery had to do more with the difficulty of changing the system rather than its evanescent superiority to the more productive system of free labor. "The most, therefore, that can be inferred from the existence of the system at present day is that it is self-supporting."[5]

Moreover, the slave system was predicated on expansionism. Economically, slavery's disdain for crop rotation and other soil conservation methods led to soil exhaustion so that an unlimited amount of fertile soil would be neces-

---

[3] An excellent review of the debate can be found in Thomas J. Pressley, Americans Interpret Their Civil War (Princeton, 1954).

[4] John E. Cairnes, The Slave Power (New York, 1969), 68. (Italics his).

[5] Cairnes, Slave Power, 69.

sary for the maintenance of the system. Too, Cairnes saw
another reason for slavery's expansionism -- the political
motive. "The desire is to obtain fresh territory for the
creation of slave states, with a view to influence in the
Senate, has carried the South in its career of aggression
far beyond the range which its mere industrial necessities
would have prescribed."[6] In fact, Cairnes argued that the
South had been so successful in increasing its supply of
fresh lands, that its most urgent need was not more virgin
soil, but more slaves to cultivate its land.

Cairnes had no difficulty in foreseeing the end of
slavery once land expansion was halted. On the one hand,
every year would see the increase in slave population; while,
on the other hand, a decrease in land suitable for cultivation would occur. The older states would be hurt first,
for as the supply of slaves increased, the price would drop
so that slave breeding would cease to be profitable. And as
the supply of land decreased, the newer slave states would
experience a drop in labor productivity so that eventually
the return on slave labor would fall below the cost of its
support. "And then," Cairnes prophesized, "the progress
toward catastrophe would be rapid."[7]

In effect, Cairnes laid down the economic foundation

---

[6] Cairnes, Slave Power, 202.

[7] Cairnes, Slave Power, 269.

for all subsequent analysis of the South as land-hungry.
His notion of the slave system as a necessary and relent-
less land-devourer appears again and again in the works
of historians writing well after the end of the Civil
War.

An equally important contributor to the economic
view of the ante-bellum South was Ulrich B. Phillips.
Phillips published his first work in 1905 -- the beginning of a career which stretched through the "progressive
era" of historical writing and hinted at the later "revisionist school" which maintained that the Civil War was a
needless war.[8]

Slavery, Phillips felt, was established by whites
for a blend of social and economic reasons: "private gain
and public safety"[9] is the phrase Phillips used repeatedly.
Yet, while the need for a slave system as a means of public

---

[8] Phillips' racism, which has made him an anathema
to later generations of scholars, was very much in tune with
the racism of the Progressive era. Further, Phillips' view
of slavery as a means of social control complemented progressive historiography.

[9] This was Phillips' feeling in 1905, but writing
in 1929, he said: "For a man to be property may seem bar-
baric and outrageous, but in this twentieth century thousands of divorced husbands are legally required to pay per-
iodic alimony to their ex-wives, and if one seeks escape
for the levy on his earnings he may be clapped into prison
until he gives adequate pledges of compliance. . . This
institution of alimony has developed somewhat unawares;
and so, in some degree did Negro slavery."   Ulrich B.
Phillips, Life and Labor in the Old South (Boston, 1963),
160.

safety or social control continued unabated, the economic
motive soon became weakened with the closing off of slave
inportation in 1807. With the supply of slaves thus limited, Phillips reasoned, the cost of owning a slave grew
and, although still lower than wages for free labor, the
difference in productivity made slave labor less economical.

For Phillips, the ratio of slave prices to cotton
prices was essential to evaluate an investment in slaves.
On the one hand, after the supply of slaves had been "cor-
nered" the price of slaves would naturally be "bid up to
the point of overvaluation."[10] And on the other hand, the
price of cotton was declining. Phillips found that between
1800 and 1860 the ratio of slave prices to cotton prices
increased more than ten times, a change which Phillips
interpreted as proof of the overvaluation of slaves. Phillips
rejected the explanation that the change in the ratio could
be primarily due to increased slave productivity; instead,
he concluded that speculation controlled slave prices.[11]
Moreover, Phillips pronounced: "This proclivity for buying
slaves was the worst feature of the regime from an economic
point of view, for it drained capital out of every develop-
ing district and froze local assets into one form of investment.[12]

10 Phillips, "The Economic Cost of Slaveholding in
the Cotton Belt," Political Science Quarterly, xx (June,
1905) 271.

11 Phillips, "Economic Cost," 269.

12 Phillips, Life and Labor, 185.

All told then, Phillips was not convinced that
"private gain" continued to be a consideration. "The re-
morseless advance of slave prices as measured in their
produce tended to spread . . . adverse conditions . . . in
all parts of the South; and by the close of the 'fifties
it is fairly certain that no slaveholders but those few
whose plantations lay in the most advantageous parts of the
cotton and sugar districts and whose managerial ability was
exceptionally great were earning anything beyond what could
cover their maintenance and carrying charges."[13]

Regarding southern expansion, Phillips was doubt-
ful. He opposed the Cairnes view on the necessity of new
lands. Instead, Phillips argued that expansion was both
impracticable and possibly damaging. Virtually all the good
cotton land was already within the borders of the South; and
if new land were practicable, the resulting increase in cultivation would increase the price of slaves and lower the
price of cotton. Further, Phillips felt "actual expansion
had in fact been too rapid for the best interests of society,
for it had kept the population too sparse to permit a proper
development of schools and agencies of communication."[14]
Hence, Phillips concluded that the importance of maintaining
the slave system lay not in its economics, but in its social

---

[13] Phillips, _American Negro Slavery_ (Baton Rouge,
1966) 391.

[14] Phillips, _American Negro_, 399.

aspect. "To the leaders in the South, with their ever-present view of the possibility of negro uprisings, the regulations of slavery seemed essential for safety and prosperity. And when they found themselves about to become powerless to check any legislation hostile to the established order in the South, they adopted the policy of secession, seeking, as they saw it, the lesser of the evils confronting them."[15]

Phillips' argument, then, questions the profitability of the slave system. Once, having examined the slave/cotton price ratio and declaring its rise due to overvaluation of slaves deriving from speculation, Phillips can assume that slave owners were not owners because of "private gain" but mainly locked in to slavery for non-economic reasons. Slavery was, in Phillips' view, a system important as an instrument for controlling a mass of black people who were inferior and incapable.

Writing a decade later, Lewis C. Gray, in his monumental study of southern agriculture, disagreed with Phillips on profitability. Tipping his hat in Phillips' direction, Gray acknowledged that by 1860 speculation might have been responsible for lifting slave prices temporarily beyond their usual ratio to cotton prices; but, he continued, it was more likely that the ratio had changed over sixty years due

[15] Phillips, "Economic Cost," 274.

to growing efficiency in the plantation system and increasing labor scarcity.[16] "In the last analysis however," Gray
concluded, "the proslavery arguments were built upon one
solid rock of truth -- slavery as an institution was justified economically . . . Under favorable conditions it was
exceedingly profitable. . . "[17]

Gray's voice was a lonely one. The decades of the
1930's and 1940's saw the development of the revisionist
school which held that the Civil War was a "repressible"
conflict as opposed to the "irrepressible" school to which
Cairnes belonged. This interpretation, which turned on the
view hinted at by Phillips, held that slavery -- as an unprofitable system -- had become moribund by 1860. Hence,
the Civil War was an unnecessary conflict caused by blunder-
ing politicians, not by the inevitable clash of two economic
systems.

The economic aspects of the argument first found
their way into print in an essay written by Charles W.
Ramsdell in 1929. For Ramsdell, it was the land expansion
question which had important economic consequences. He did
not believe, as many historians have thought, that a shortage
of land would doom slavery. Like Phillips, his forecast of
doom was based on the abundance of land for cotton cultivation. The cultivation of this land, in the Southwest, would

---

[16] Lewis C. Gray, History of Agriculture in the
Southern United States to 1860 (2 vols, New York, 1941) II, 667.

[17] Gray, History, 939-940.

have meant an "over production" of cotton and consequent drop in the price of cotton. "Even on better lands," Ramsdell argued, "the margin of profit would have declined. Prices of slaves must have dropped then, even in the southwest; importation from border states would have fallen off; thousands of slaves would have become not only unprofitable but a heavy burden, the market for them gone."[18]

Hence, according to Ramsdell, the South was hoist by its own petard. On the one hand, cotton cultivation was only profitable if there were vast amounts of fertile land and the price of cotton remained high. Yet, on the other hand, the greater the amount of cotton cultivation, the larger the supply of cotton, and the lower the price of cotton. This economic vise hypothesized by Ramsdell began to tighten by 1857. And the "natural limits" had been reached by 1860. The Civil War, then, having been fought over the question of territorial expansion was premature; for, Ramsdell believed, "had not the war intervened, there is every reason to believe that there would have been a continuous overproduction and very low prices throughout the sixties and seventies."[19] In fact, Ramsdell concluded that the "natural " destruction of slavery would have occurred in

---

[18] Charles W. Ramsdell, "The Natural Limits of Slavery Expansion," Mississippi Valley Historical Review, 16 (September, 1929), 169-170.

[19] Ramsdell, "Natural Limits," 169.

"perhaps a generation, probably less."[20]

As we have seen, Phillips' writing on the ante-
bellum South signalled a new attitude not only toward the
South, but toward slavery. While Phillips did not contend
that slavery was about to die because of the slave/cotton
price ration, he opened the door to, in his words, a "more
satisfactory analysis" which usually took the form of plantation studies, in consequence, records of plantations were
combed for estimates of profitability. One such important
study was Charles S. Sydnor's study of Mississippi. And
where Phillips hesitated at the threshold Sydnor walked
on through to declare slavery unprofitable.

Sydnor's investigation applied accounting methods to
a Mississippi plantation of the 1850's engaged in cotton
production with the labor of 50 slaves. He calculated that
" . . . 50 slaves, at $600 each . . . represented an invest-
ment of $30,000. Calculating interest at 6%, this amounted
to $1800."[21] He added an equal amount for depreciation.
For the investment in land, Sydnor figured that 600 acres
would be sufficient. "Allowing $10 per acre, the investment
in land at 6% interest involved a yearly carriage charge
of $360, and it ordinarily depreciated at a rate of at least
3% a year in value (or) $180."[22] Sydnor then added $300 for

---

[20] Ramsdell, Natural Limits," 171.

[21] Charles S. Sydnor, <u>Slavery in Mississippi</u>, (New
York, 1933), 196.

[22] Sydnor, <u>Slavery</u>, 196.

the yearly wage of an overseer and $1000 for miscellaneous

plantation supplies. "The total of the expenses and interest

charges was $5440" which, when subtracted from the total

yearly income from cotton sales of $6320, yielded a profit

for the planter of $880.[23] And this, Sydnor felt, was an

optimistic figure.

Sydnor argued that plantation owners probably would

have been better off economically without slavery and that,

in fact, ". . . many Mississippi planters prospered in spite

of slavery because cotton was profitable and land cheap."[24]

Moreover, Sydnor contended that whatever "soundness" Missis-

sippi's investment in slaves possessed was dependent on the

price of slaves -- any drop in the price would have been

disasterous for the state. Much like Ramsdell, Sydnor found

Mississippi caught in an economic bind, but unlike Ramsdell,

Sydnor thought that territorial expansion was the only way out:

> Considering the price of slaves and of cotton,
> it was impossible for a planter to make large
> profits and many of them lost heavily . . .
> By 1860 Mississippi had nearly as many slaves
> as it needed. With the natural increase in
> slave population the price must have declined
> unless a market for the surplus could be found.
> Texas for a time could buy from Mississippi as
> Mississippi had for years bought from Virginia,
> but when Texas and the rest of the Southwest

---

[23] Sydnor, Slavery, 197.

[24] Sydnor, Slavery, 199.

> were supplied, slave prices would fall unless
> more territory suited to slave labor could be
> discovered. [25]

Hence, Sydnor concluded, slave owners had to be expansionist
in order to keep up the price of their slaves.

Another follower of Phillips, but one who goes in
quite a different direction than Sydnor, is Eugene Genovese.
For Genovese, the antebellum South was moving closer and
closer to a crisis. This crisis had its origins in the
economic system of slavery: it is simply that a slave economy was so inefficient when pitted against the capitalist
North, that the South slipped further and further behind the
North. The only hope for the South was through territorial
expansion.

Genovese argued that inherent in a slave economy
were "irrational tendencies." These tendencies, such as
labor force inefficiencies and lack of cheap free white labor,
inhibited economic development. Moreover, there was a tendency
for slave owners to engage in heavy conspicuous consumption
rather than saving as required for growth. Along with a
stagnant economy, the South was rapidly depleting its lands,
and its "inability to combat soil exhaustion effectively
proved one of the most serious economic features of its general crisis."[26] Compounding the crisis of soil depletion was

---

[25] Sydnor, _Slavery_, 202.

[26] Eugene Genovese, _The Political Economy of Slavery_
(New York, 1965), 85.

the fact that agricultural reform in the old South depended on wasteful farming methods in the new South --
depended, in other words, on the plantation system of gang
labor to create markets for the sale of surplus slaves
which raised capital and reduced the labor force in the old
South. Thus, ". . . a general reformation of southern agriculture could not take place while slavery was retained."[27]

Since the planter aristocracy which ruled the South
was, according to Genovese, firmly attached to the social
institutions grown around the slave system, discarding
slavery was not an option. "No solution emerged from within
the system, but one beckoned from without. The steady acquisition of new land could alone guarantee the maintenance of
the interregional slave trade which held the system together."[28] Of course, Genovese argued that expansion had political goals as well: most obviously, maintaining southern parity in the Senate.

For Genovese, the question of profitability had
little importance. "The planter typically recoiled at the
notion that profit should be the goal of life; that the
approach to production and exhange should be internally

---

[27] Genovese, _Political Economy_, 144.

[28] Genovese, _Political Economy_, 247.

rational and uncomplicated by social values. . . "[29] In
fact, at the end of his essay on the political economy of
slavery, Genovese argued that a sensible scenario could be
written which would sustain either repressibility or irrepressibility of the Civil War, or the profitability or
unprofitability of slavery. "Great social transformations
do not come about as a result of a kind of popular income
accounting. An accurate knowledge of profit and loss will
not tell us much about the origins of the secession crisis,"
he concluded.[30]

Most historians would disagree. The question of
profitability is an important one; especially since the
issue of profitability, once settled, aids in settling a
larger class of questions related to the economic causes of
the Civil War. For example, the revisionist interpretation
that the Civil War was "unnecessary" because slavery would
have died a natural death surely depends on the notion that
the slave system was headed for economic collapse. If the
slave system is shown to have been economically healthy, i.e.,
that it was and would continue to be profitable to rear and
keep slaves, the likelihood of its impending natural death
may be dismissed. By the same token, those interpretations
of the causes of the Civil War which have the conflict

[29] Genovese, <u>Political Economy</u>, 28.

[30] Genovese, <u>Political Economy</u>, 282.

irrepressible depend on the notion that two economic systems
were at stake. If one of those systems, slavery, can be
shown to have been on the verge of self-destruction, the
case for irrepressibility must suffer. Hence, as Gavin Wright
argued above, the question of profitability is a relevant
one indeed.

The profitability issue is also a question which
has long divided historians. For the question itself has
proved to be an extremely slippery one and its exact formulation open to disagreement. Probably a classic instance
of confusion over the formulation of the question of profitability was shown by Charles Sydnor. According to Sydnor's
accounting figures, the apparent rate of return on an investment in a plantation was a tiny 2.4% -- well below the
rate of return in alternative investments during the period.[31]
However, Thomas Govan and Kenneth Stampp have both quite
correctly criticized Sydnor's accounting techniques. The
usual accounting procedure includes interest as part of profits -- not, as Sydnor did, as an expense.[32] Thus, correcting Sydnor's error of subtracting the interest charges for
the capital value of land and slaves from gross income,

[31] Robert Fogel and Stanley Engerman, "The Economics
of Slavery," in Robert Fogel and Stanley Engerman, eds.,
The Reinterpretation of American Economic History (New York,
1971) 321.

[32] Thomas P. Govan, "Was Plantation Slavery Profitable?" Journal of Southern History, VIII (1942) 527. Kenneth
M. Stampp, Peculiar Institution (New York, 1956) 404.

would raise the rate of return from 2.4% to 8.4%.[33] Govan
and Stampp also pointed out that Sydnor omitted the capital
gain from reproduction of slaves and the increased value of
existing slaves from his estimate of plantation income.
Modern economic analysis would confirm the Govan-Stampp
criticism of the omission of capital gains from slave reproduction; whether one should include unanticipated capital
gains on existing slaves is debatable.

Govan's own estimate of the rate of return on three
plantations in the old South, between 1841 and 1853, ranged
from 6.6%, 6.9% and 12%,[34] figures which led him ". . . to
the tentative conclusion that the students who have stated
that slavery was profitable are more nearly correct than
those who deny its profitability."[35] Similarly, Stampp
argued that ". . . there is ample evidence that the average
slaveholder earned a reasonably satisfactory return upon his
investment in slaves."[36]

Stampp also ran through other arguments which have
been advanced to prove slavery unprofitable. He argued
that the presence of indebtedness meant nothing more than,
at worst, managerial inefficiency or lack of regard for

---

[33] Fogel and Engerman, "Economics of Slavery," 322.

[34] Govan, "Was Plantation Slavery?" 531.

[35] Govan, "Was Plantation Slavery?" 535.

[36] Stampp, Peculiar Institution, 404.

middle-class notions of thrift; and at best, indebtedness
to enlarge agricultural operations was good business if
the initial investment was sound. Further, Stampp discarded
the notion that slavery was the cause of soil exhaustion:
he reasoned that in a situation where land was cheap and
labor so dear, it made sense to use labor at the expense of
land. Stampp argued that since cotton was the South's
comparative advantage, the fact that its economy depended on
cotton was not a sign of lopsided economic development. So
too, slavery had a competitive advantage over free white
labor in the production of cotton. And finally, looking
at hire rates for slaves, Stampp concluded ". . . the high
valuation of Negro labor during the 1850's was the best and
most direct evidence of the continued profitability of
slavery."[37]

Thus, as we have seen, there is no consensus among
historians on the profitability issue. On the one side,
there were those like Cairnes, Phillips, Ramsdell, Sydnor
and Genovese who believed that the slave system was headed
for an economic crisis of one sort or another. On the other
side, historians like Gray, Stampp and Govan heartily disagreed. And, with arguments on both sides of the profitability question, there can be no agreement, either, on the

---

[37] Stampp, Peculiar Institution, 391-414.

economic causes of the Civil War. These disagreements
have, of course, led historians themselves to speculate.
Stampp has suggested he is untroubled by these uncertainties and looks forward to the continuing debate over the
causes of the Civil War.[38] Similarly, Don Fehrenbacher
feels "it is obvious that the final word will never be
written, for each generation of Americans discovers some
new understanding of itself in studying the era of the
Civil War."[39] A position characterized by another historian, Thomas Pressley, as one which "does not provide much
warmth for the ego of the historian."[40]

However lightheatedly historians might view the
uncertainties which often punctuate their profession, it
must still be admitted that some particular questions, like
whether slavery was profitable, call out for more objective
formulation and answer. In fact, the question of profitability is more tractable than the discussion so far has indicated.

Much of the tractability this issue possesses is
due to that new generation of economic historians armed with

---

[38] Kenneth M. Stampp, The Causes of the Civil War
(Englewood Cliffs, New Jersey, 1959) vi.

[39] Don Fehrenbacher, "Disunion and Reunion," in
John Higham, The Reconstruction of American History (New
York, 1962) 118.

[40] Pressley, Americans Interpret, 12.

a sophisticated grasp of both economic theory and mathe-
matics.[41] What distinguishes these new economic historians
from the old is, quite simply, the notion that for the purposes of analyzing their impact on the economy, slaves can
be viewed as machinery in the production of cotton and
other agricultural goods. Slaves, in other words, were
a sort of capital good. In the context of the southern agricultural system, the purchase and use of slaves resembled
more that of capital than that of labor. Like machines,
slaves were purchased for use over a long period of time, a
lump sum was paid for future services; like machines slaves
wore out and, in the case of children, purchase may have
involved a period before capital contributed to output. Like
machines, a thriving market existed for the lease of slaves.
And finally, like machines, slaves had to be maintained by
their purchaser.[42] Thus, an investment in slaves can be
viewed as an investment decision subject to the same economic
considerations as other investment decisions -- such as the
purchase of railroad rolling stock or steam engines. This

---

[41] For an explanation of the new economic history,
See Stuart Bruchey's Introduction to The Roots of American
Economic Growth; and Robert Fogel's "The New Economic His-
tory, Its Findings and Methods," Economic History Review,
XIX (December 1966).

[42] A confusing aspect of this parallel is the fact
that slaves can reproduce themselves. Much discussion has
gone on about slave reproduction, as we shall see. However,
from the standpoint of capital theory, this distinction is
not important since there are machines which are used to
produce other machines.

notion of slavery freed economic historians from the old
constraints of judging the success of the slave system
through plantation accounts, or primarily as a moral question.[43] Instead, the analysis of slavery became subject to
scrutiny through the principles of capital theory.

The increased power and rigor in organizing the
profitability issue is at once obvious in the new economic
historians' criticisms of the old. Phillips' use of the
slave/cotton price ratio as a measure of profitability has
been questioned, for example, by new economic historians
Robert Fogel and Stanley Engerman. Phillips, without offer-
ing evidence, asserted that the rise in the slave/cotton
price ratio was caused by speculation or "frenzied finance"
made possible because the supply of slaves had been "cor-
nered." However, as Fogel and Engerman point out, the
existence of a corner depends on monopolistic control of all

---

[43] The attempt to treat slavery apart from various
moral categories -- not the least of which is the treatment
of slaves as a capital good -- has come under attack from
some old economic historians. In response to that criticism,
Alfred Conrad has argued: "What concerns me most is the
notion that if you name a number of things that must prove
slavery is bad, then, if it was bad, it cannot have been
profitable. It is not necessary that we believe evil states
are unprofitable or inefficient in order to remain moral
men. We seem to come back all the time to the idea that,
because slavery was evil, it must also have been inefficient.
I don't believe that. The sooner we start to make these
distinctions, the sooner will we be able to deal with the
evil things in this world." Alfred Conrad, Douglas Dowd,
Stanley Engerman, et. al., "Slavery as an Obstacle to
Economic Growth in the United States: A Panel Discussion,"
Journal of Economic History, XXVII (December, 1967) 557.

or most of the supply of slaves. Yet, the slave market was
composed of many thousands of slave owners, none of whom
ever controlled more than a small part of the supply of slaves.
"Phillips confused the concept of monopoly, which gives a
seller control over the market price, with the existence of
an inelastic and relatively fixed short-run supply. The ban
on the African trade did not give a particular group of planters control over the price of slaves. Rather, it made the
short-run supply curve of slave labor inelastic and limited
the rate at which the stock of slave labor could increase to
the natural rate of increase of the domestic slave population.[44]

Ramsdell, too, suffers from the scrutiny of Fogel
and Engerman. In Ramsdell's analysis, the overproduction of
cotton, and its consequent drop in price, would have eventually
spelled doom for slavery. Of course, even if the supply of
cotton had increased enormously and the demand for cotton had
kept pace with the supply, a good price for cotton would have
been maintained. Ramsdell, however, never explored that
possibility; Fogel and Engerman did. Ramsdell's prediction
about the continued fall in the price of cotton was based on
the fact that in 1858, 1859 and 1860, the price of cotton
dropped steadily from its 1857 price. But, as Fogel and
Engerman pointed out, the 1857 price was "unusually high";

---

[44] Fogel and Engerman, "Economics of Slavery,"
313.

". . . the average real price of 1858-1860 equalled or
exceeded the average of all but one of the other three-
year periods between 1840 and 1860 . . . "[45] According
to Fogel and Engerman, Ramsdell misinterpreted the significance of the advance in 1857 and decline thereafter
as the result of increased cotton production or increased
supply. "Quite the contrary," argue Fogel and Engerman,
"the sharp rise in output after 1857 was a lagged response
to substantial increase in demand. Despite the probable
increase in the amount of land devoted to cotton during
these years, and the substantial rise in the output of
cotton that accompanied it, the supply of cotton did not
increase rapidly enough to reduce the price to its earlier
level. In 1860 the real price of cotton was still sub-
stantially above the average of the previous two decades."[46]

Another historian to suffer from the new methods is
Eugene Genovese. Genovese's interpretation of the antebellum
period has come under attack from all sides,[47] and almost
every economic argument made by Genovese has been criticized.
Southern economic development, characterized by Genovese as

---

[45] Fogel and Engerman, "Economics of Slavery," 317.

[46] Fogel and Engerman, "Economics of Slavery," 318.

[47] See especially Lee Benson, Toward the Scientific
Study of History (New York, 1972) 226-270.

stagnant, has been described as "thriving" and "growing" by Fogel and Engerman; the gloomy short-run and long-run prospects of slavery that Genovese saw have proved to be quite the contrary; profitability is still considered a central point; and the necessity of land expansion argued by Genovese has been undercut by arguments showing that there was no land shortage in the South on the eve of the Civil War and that land expansion might, in fact, have harmed the southern economy.[48]

But it is on the issue of profitability that Genovese has been most battered.[49] Even taken at its most general level, his argument that profitability is not an important question, is a shaky one. Genovese's notion of owning slaves not for profit's sake but as "badges of honor, prestige and power" is the basis of his argument that slavery generated social institutions which were distinct from the North. If it were true that slave prices did not reflect the value of

---

[48] For example, Fogel and Engerman, "Economics of Slavery," 333-336; Gavin Wright, "New and Old Views on the Economics of Slavery," JEH, XXXIII (June, 1973), 460-463. Although, on the question of just how gloomy slave owners felt on the eve of the Civil War, Genovese has backtracked a bit; see Stanley Engerman, Robert Fogel, Eugene Genovese and Herbert Gutman, "New Directions in Black History: A Symposium," (The University of Rochester) forum, (Spring, 1972) 22-47.

[49] See below for a discussion of the findings of the new economic history.

slave labor, then Genovese might infer correctly that slave owners were not strictly economic men, and indirectly find support for the notion that the social institutions which proceeded from the slave system were as essential to the market value of slaves as the economics. But if it can be shown that slave purchases could be justified strictly on the motive of maximizing business profits, then the rest of Genovese's case collapses. For, if slave use can be shown to have been a profitable endeavor, then one might just as well argue that slave owners were rational businessmen and their fight to uphold the slave system was a reasonable response to considerations of economic self-interest.

The real value of the new economic history lies, of course, not in its criticisms of the work of the old, but in the answers it can generate by its more power methodology. The pioneer work in the new approach to the profitability of slavery was an essay, published in 1958, by Alfred Conrad and John Meyer. They lamented that "no attempt has ever been made to measure the profitability of slavery according to the economic (as opposed to accounting) concept of profitability," and said, "specifically, we shall attempt to measure the profitability of southern slave operations in terms of modern capital theory."[50]

---

[50] Alfred Conrad and John Meyer, "The Economics of Slavery in the Ante-Bellum South," in Fogel and Engerman, eds., The Reinterpretation, 343.

Conrad and Meyer set out, then, to evaluate the rate of return earned on an investment in slaves. The first step toward evaluation involved finding the marginal physical product of slaves. For this, Conrad and Meyer set forth two production functions, or two ways of relating inputs to output, which in this case meant (1) a production function to calculate the relationship of the output of southern staple crops, especially cotton, to the inputs of slaves and material for slave-maintenance; and (2) a function to describe the production, or output, of more slaves by female slaves (procreation). With information gained from the production functions, along with data on slave and cotton prices, Conrad and Meyer were able to estimate the annual net income accruing to slave owners. This procedure involves multiplying the figures on the additional cotton produced by an extra slave by the price of cotton per pound, which yields the gross revenue attributable to that extra slave. From gross revenue, Conrad and Meyer deducted the cost of slave maintenance to get an annual net revenue accruing to a slave owner from the slave's labor. The net revenue over the lift-time of the slave gave Conrad and Meyer a life-time income stream, which could then be compared with the purchase price of the slave to determine the rate of return on an initial investment in slaves. It was this rate of return that Conrad and Meyer than compared to rates of return on alternative investments available in the capital market to determine whether an investment in slaves was good business.

This procedure required Conrad and Meyer to estimate
values for many variables, such as annual returns from slave
labor for both field work and procreation and interest
rates on alternative investments outside slave-run southern
agriculture.[51] As we have seen, the net revenue of a male
field hand depended on maintenance cost, the price of cotton
and the quantity of his annual output. Annual output, of
course, is tied primarily to the quality of the land being
worked. Thus, Conrad and Meyer hypothesized 12 cases of
differing capital outlays, from the best lands of the southwest to the poorest lands of the eastern seaboard, and got
annual returns varying from 4.5% to 13%. They concluded:
"These first six cases, with returns ranging from 4½ and 8
percent, encompass the majority of antebellum cotton plantation operations."[52] For the production function involving
female slaves, Conrad and Meyer added in the labor productivity of her children and the returns realized from their sale,
and subtracted out the extra cost of maternity and of maintaining the children. For a mother bearing ten children,
the hypothesized upper limit, Conrad and Meyer obtained a
rate of return of 8.1%; for a mother bearing five children,

---

[51] Conrad and Meyer, "Slavery in the Ante-Bellum
South," 344.

[52] Conrad and Meyer, "Slavery in the Ante-Bellum
South," 349.

the lower limit, the return was 7.1%.[53]

Conrad and Meyer's estimate of alternative rates
of return takes into account the wholesale withdrawal of
capital from slave-run southern agriculture. They estimated
that such a withdrawal would not have depressed marginal
investment returns much below 4.5 to 5%; and that the
withdrawn capital would not have earned much more than 8%.
Between these two estimates, Conrad and Meyer chose a
return of 6% for comparison with returns on slave investments.[54]

Comparing returns on slaves which ranged from 4½%
to 8.1% to returns of 6% on other investments, Conrad and
Meyer concluded: ". . . slavery was apparently as remunera-
tive as alternative employments to which slave capital might
have been put. Large or excessive returns were clearly
limited to a few fortunate planters, but apparently none
suffered excessively either."[55] Yet, Conrad and Meyer continued, without the market mechanism to insure that slaves bred
and reared on the least productive land could be sold to
those owning the most productive land, slavery could not be

---

[53] Conrad and Meyer, "Slavery in the Ante-Bellum
South," 349-350.

[54] Conrad and Meyer, "Slavery in the Ante-Bellum
South," 346-347.

[55] Conrad and Meyer, "Slavery in the Ante-Bellum
South," 351.

considered profitable. Profitability, then, depended on
the efficient production and transfer of slaves from one area
to another. Looking at the demographic profile of slavery
in the old South and new South, Conrad and Meyer found clear
evidence that " . . . the old South recognized its function
as the slave-breeding area for the cotton-raising West."[56]

  Thus, in Conrad and Meyer's view, the entire South
profited from slavery. The rate of return on slave labor in
the cotton belt was high, and the demand for slaves in the
southwest insured high returns to "breeding operations" in
the southeastern states. While the methods of the new
economic history represent a startling departure from the
methods, and often the opinions, of the old history, Conrad
and Meyer echo the mainstream opinion on the land expansion
question. They concluded: "Continued expansion of slave
territory was both possible and, to some extent, necessary.
The maintenance of profits in the old South depended upon
the expansion, extensive or intensive, of slave agriculture
into the southwest. This is sufficient to explain the interest of the old South in secession and does away with the
necessity to fall back upon arguments of statesmanship or
quixotism to explain the willingness to fight for the peculiar

---

  [56] Conrad and Meyer, "Slavery in the Ante-Bellum
South," 356.

institution."[57]

Like most pioneering works, the Conrad and Meyer
essay has been criticized quite roundly. Most of those
criticisms are aimed at the structure of the argument. For
example, Fogel and Engerman point out that Conrad and Meyer
did not provide an estimate of the average rate of return
actually earned by investors during 1830-1860. To interpret
their estimates as actual earnings would be impossible
because, for slaves purchased in the late years, the Civil
War intervened before the expected returns could be realized;
and, for slaves purchased before 1835, the real purchase
price was lower than the one Conrad and Meyer used in their
analysis. Rather, Conrad and Meyer's estimates show that
" . . . a person who purchased a prime slave during 1846-
1850 at the prevailing market price could, if he based himself
on recent experience, expect to earn about the same rate of
return on his investment in slaves as was being earned on
alternative long-term investment opportunities."[58] In other
words, business considerations alone justified 1846-1850
slave prices; thus, Phillips' assertion that slave prices
were inflated by speculation or overvalued because of conspicuous consumption was unfounded.

---

[57] Conrad and Meyer, "Slavery in the Ante-Bellum
South," 360.

[58] Fogel and Engerman, "Economics of Slavery," 323.

Four years after Conrad and Meyer published their
essay, Robert Evans, Jr., published his study of slavery.
Asking the same question as Conrad and Meyer, but using a
more sophisticated method, Evans' analysis confirmed for
1830-1860 what Conrad and Meyer had found to be true for
1846-1850. The most important refinement in Evans' work was
his use of the annual rental or hire price of slaves to estimate their annual net earnings. As Evans explained: "This
method uses net rent, received by owners of slaves when they
rented them out, as the estimate of the income earned by the
capital good. Stated more formally, the analysis is limited
to a firm with one input, a single form of capital, which
produces a single output, labor services."[59] This approach
enabled Evans to estimate income figures directly from
market data and to avoid the many estimating problems which
faced Conrad and Meyer.

Evans' discount formula used four types of data:
(1) the net yearly income received by the owner of 1000 male
slaves -- buying them at age 20, holding them for 20 or 30
years and selling them --; (2) the price of slaves; (3) the
death rate of slaves at specific ages; (4) rates of return
on alternative investments. Evans used the standard equation

---

[59] Robert Evans, Jr., "The Economics of American
Negro Slavery, 1830-1860," Aspects of Labor Economics (Princeton, 1962) 191.

for estimating the rate of return but took into account the
probability that the asset (slave) disappeared (died)
during a given year. Also, separate rates of return for
slaves in the upper South and lower South were calculated.

Evans found that for the upper South, rates of
return from 1830-1860 ranged from 9.5 to 14.3%. For the
lower South, rates of return ranged from 10.3 to 18.5%.[60]
When compared to rates of return of alternative investments
such as Boston railroad stock and manufacturing stocks,
which Evans found averaged arount 10%, Evans conservatively
concluded that "the rates of return on slave capital for the
period 1830 through 1860 were at least equal to the rates of
return being received on alternative forms of capital."[61]

The interpretation of Evans' results suffered the
same fate as those of Conrad and Meyer. Again, Evans did not
provide estimates of the average rates of return _actually_
earned by slave owners. Evans' analysis assumed that the
average hire rate prevailing in the year the slave was purchased would remain the same throughout the period the slave
was held; in fact, the average hire rate rose sharply from
1835 on, as did the price of slaves during the 1850's but
which, again, Evans' analysis kept static. That is, no allow-
ance for change was made between the time of purchase and the

---

[60] Evans, "Negro Slavery," 217.

[61] Evans, "Negro Slavery," 221.

time of potential sale. Yet, as with Conrad and Meyer, Evans' findings do show that business considerations alone were sufficient to explain slave prices: expected rates of returns were equal to, or above, returns in alternative investments.

While Evans' findings were in harmony with Conrad and Meyer's results, a final agreement on the investment soundness of slave labor was not forthcoming. These disagreements, however, revolved around alternative uses of data rather than fundamental conflicts on methods of estimation. In 1964 Edward Saraydar published criticisms of Conrad and Meyer's estimates for the average physical product of male slaves and average capital cost per slave. Not content with the opinions of contemporary observers on slave productivity -- as were Conrad and Meyer -- Saraydar estimated slave productivity from the 1850 Census. Using a sample of counties, Saraydar totalled both the cotton production and number of slaves; he divided the number of slaves into the number of cotton bales and got the number of bales produced per slave. Saraydar reasoned that only half the total number of slaves were involved in cotton production, so he multiplied by two the number of bales per slave which resulted in an estimate of 3.2 bales as the cotton output per prime male field hand. This figure was lower than the 3.75 bales of Conrad and Meyer. With this lower estimate of productivity Saraydar went back to Conrad and Meyer's equation and recal-

culated the net earnings of a slave, obtaining a lower
estimate than that obtained by Conrad and Meyer. Saraydar
also increased the estimate of the capital cost per slave.
These two changes in the calculation of the rate of return
resulted in rates varying from .025% to 8.2% -- but mostly
less than 6%. Thus, Saraydar concluded that: ". . . contrary to Conrad and Meyer's conclusion, antebellum cotton
production under the slave system generally failed to earn
returns which were in any sense comparable to a 'normal'
return of say 6% . . . "[62]

Saraydar's estimates, in turn, have been criticized
by Richard Sutch. According to Sutch, Saraydar made two
crucial errors: (1) he neglected the income associated with
slave reproduction and (2) he underestimated slave productivity. For the first, Sutch calculated the impact of reproduction and found the effects on profitability estimates to
be significant but not sufficient to boost the rate of
return above 6%. In regard to Saraydar's second error,
Sutch argued that a productivity estimate based on cotton
production in 1849 (the Census of 1850) was hardly unbiased
because 1849 had been a year of particularly bad crops. Instead, Sutch recalculated slave productivity using data on
cotton production from the 1860 Census. Moreover, Stuch
observed that when Saraydar divided cotton output by the

---

[62] Edward Sarydar, "A Note on the Profitability of
Ante-Bellum Slavery," Southern Economic Journal, 30 (April,
1964) 331.

number of slaves the result is <u>not</u> product per prime male
hand but per slave worker. A result which underestimates
product per prime male hand since women, children and men
over 50 years composed over half of the labor force. Sutch's
results show that ". . . cotton production was clearly profitable for the alluvial or prairie lands of the New South,
when compared with the 6% alternative interest rate."[63]

Undoubtedly both Saraydar's and Sutch's approach to
slave productivity was an improvement over Conrad and Meyer.
And in 1970 James Foust and Dale Swan published a study
which represented a further improvement in estimating productivity. While Saraydar and Sutch relied on published
Census data, Foust and Swan used the manuscript of the
census for 1850 and 1860; they eliminated cotton produced
on farms which had no slave labor and included farmers and
farmers' sons who worked alongside slaves in cotton production. Their estimate of bales per slave laborer, assuming
a participation rate of 50% field hands, was 3.18 in 1849
and 4.44 in 1859.[64]

---

[63] Richard Sutch, "The Profitability of Ante-Bellum
Slavery Revised," Southern Economic Journal, 30 (April, 1965),
375.

[64] James Foust and Dale Swan, "Productivity and Profitability of Antebellum Slave Labor: A Micro Approach," Agricultural History, 44 (January, 1970), 44-46. Another study
measuring productivity is Raymond Battalio and John Kagel,
"The Structure of Antebellum Southern Agriculture: South
Carolina, a Case Study," Agricultural History, 44 (January,
1970) 25-37.

Using these estimates of productivity, Foust and
Swan went on to determine the rates of return on slaveowning,
cotton-producing plantations. Foust and Swan found that:
"Taking into account all profitable activities, including
breeding operations and the production of noncotton surplus,
clearly suggests that all regions were experiencing rates
of return in excess of the alternative rate of 6% in 1849."[65]
For 1859, Foust and Swan observed a slight drop in the average
returns for the South, but not enough to put returns below
the 6% opportunity cost of capital.

Fogel and Engerman too made a contribution to slave
productivity estimates. They observed that the Saraydar-
Foust-Swan estimates of output per average slave hand contained
downward biases which, when corrected, yielded a figure of 4.8
bales. If 4.8 bales is then multiplied by 1.3 -- the figure
they estimated would convert the product per average slave
hand into the product per prime field hand -- the result is
6.2 bales.[66] The force of evidence, thus, indicates that
Conrad and Meyer, rather than overestimating slave productivity,
underestimated it, a fact which would only raise the estimated
rate of return on slave investment.

Whatever the exact measure for slave productivity,
Conrad and Meyer, Evans, Sutch, Foust and Swan all agree: an

---

[65] Foust and Swan, "Productivity," 55.

[66] Fogel and Engerman, "Economics of Slavery," 327.

investment in slaves was a profitable one indeed. One need
look no further than the notion of good business to justify
slave ownership.

Yet, judgments on the profitability of slavery are
not crucial in determining the economic health of the slave
system. The measure of economic health is its viability.
A system is viable if there is an economic incentive to
continue it. Conversely, a non-viable system is one which,
from the point of view of the decision-makers, has become too
costly to continue.

The first test of the viability of the slave system
was offered by Yasukitichi Yasuba.[67] Yasuba argued that
viability could be determined simply by asking whether or
not there was a market for slave babies. If a slave's earnings over his or her lifetime were sufficient to cover the
rearing costs, there would be economic incentives to increase
the slave population; if slave earnings were not sufficient
to cover rearing costs, then nobody would buy or keep slave
babies. For the test of viability in these terms, Yasuba
looked at the capitalized rent in the market price of slaves.

This capitalized rent is the surplus a slave
generates for its owner over the slave's life-time, discounted
back to the present. For the first years of a slave's life,

---

[67] Robert Evans and Richard Sutch have offered
tests of viability. See Evans, "Negro Slavery," 221-226;
and Sutch, "Profitability Revisited," 365-366.

net annual outlays involved in rearing are negative --
maintaining the slave baby obviously costs more than
the slave produces. For the middle period of a slave's
life, when a slave earns more than he or she costs to
maintain, the net annual income becomes positive. During
the last years of a slave's life, old age and decreased
productivity probably return the net income to negative
figures. When all these positive and negative figures
are discounted back, the final figure will determine
whether or not the income of a slave justifies buying or
rearing that slave from birth. If the capitalized rent
on a slave at birth is positive, any number over zero,
then the slave baby will earn more than it costs to rear
and maintain. Put in another way, a businessman motivated
solely by profit would be willing to raise the baby for
personal use or later sale.

     Yasuba thus proceeded to calculate the cost
of producing an 18-year-old male slave. He found that from
1820 to 1860, the rearing cost fell far short of the market
price for slaves. In fact, looking at the trend of capitalized rents over that 40 year period, Yasuba found a constant
increase. "Thus," he concluded, "in the ante-bellum South,

slavery steadily strengthened its economic position."[68]

Yasuba's study is an impressive addition to the
findings of Conrad and Meyer, Evans, Sutch, Foust and Swan.
The evidence that slavery was solidly profitable is substantial,[69] and Yasuba's findings also indicate that slavery
was economically viable during the 40 years prior to the
Civil War. The evidence, thus, demonstrates that on the eve
of the Civil War slavery was a sound and thriving system.
Any arguments over the cause of the Civil War which hinge
on the unprofitability of slavery or the non-viability of
the slave system may be put aside with a major degree of
confidence.

Of course, some historians would quarrel with the

---

[68] Yasukichi Yasuba, "The Profitability and
Viability of Plantation Slavery in the United States,"
in Fogel and Engerman, The Reinterpretation, 367. The
Yasuba test of viability bypasses another, more fundamental, test. Even if slaves have a positive value at birth,
slavery might be non-viable -- the system would tend to
self-destruct -- if it would pay to permit slaves to buy
their freedom. We do not know if the slave system might
have eventually succumbed in this way. There is no evidence,
however, that such a test has much relevance for the ante-
bellum economy. See Robert Fogel and Stanley Engerman,
Time on the Cross (Boston, 1974), Vol. I, Chapter 6.

[69] There is however a new economic historian who
disagrees with these findings. Noel Butlin, in a critique
claims that his recalculations show slavery to have been
neither profitable nor viable. Noel Butlin, Ante-Bellum
Slavery (Canberra, Australia, 1971). Butlin has been re-
futed by Gavin Wright in New and Old Views," 454-458.

evidence generated by the new economic history. They are
suspicious of evidence generated mostly by models and numbers.
Many historians, faced with the novel and unorthodox methods
of the new economic history, would agree with Morton Rothstein's observation that: "Some practitioners of the new
art seem unwilling to undertake that careful search for data
in existing sources that is the hallmark of historical
scholarship. Rather, they are more interested in subjecting
the data used in the very works they are discrediting to
testing and manipulation with their new tools and models.[70]

Along with the reluctance of some new economic
historians to engage in grubby fact-finding, there are other
grounds for scepticism about their work. One can question
the applicability of simple, competitive economic models to
long-term historical problems like antebellum slavery. And
surely one can wonder about the explanatory power of economic
variables for historical problems in causality. But, one
cannot doubt the effectiveness of the new methods in testing
intuitive hypotheses or formulating and checking the implicit
models of the old history. Moreover, as Gavin Wright pointed
out: "The more traditional forms of 'literary' evidence are
notoriously unreliable, often subject to a multitude of interpretations . . . Where subjective choice is the only guide,

---

[70] Morton Rothstein, "The Cotton Frontier of the
Antebellum South: A Methodological Battleground," _Agricul-
tural History_, 40 (January, 1970) 154.

historians will surely differ in their decisions as to which
quotations and examples are relevant. Indeed, one of the
strongest points in favor of the use of quantitative methods
is that they often represent the only way in which historical
arguments can be settled."[71] And that is certainly true of
the profitability question.

---

[71] Gavin Wright, "The Economics of Cotton in the
Antebellum South," unpublished dissertation, Yale University, 1969, Chapter VII, 4.

CHAPTER II

THE ECONOMICS OF WESTWARD EXPANSION

New economic historians have some reason for
satisfaction. Their contribution to the debate about the
inevitability of the Civil War appears to have settled a
question that more traditional historians had been arguing
about for a century. Modern social science techniques
have made possible an assessment of the profitability and
viability of slavery. We can now pronounce, with a great
deal of confidence, (1) that slavery was a profitable business -- by any definition -- for those who owned slave labor;
(2) that the slave system was a viable one. Thus, any interpretation of the antebellum period or of the Civil War which
hinges on the unprofitability may be finally set aside.
Surely no small accomplishment for a field so young.

There are, however, other questions about the decades
preceding the Civil War which remain unanswered, and are
subject to analysis with new techniques. This thesis will
explore one of those questions -- the economic impact of the
expansion of slavery into new lands. Actually, this is not
a question in the sense that most new and traditional historians are om disagreement. They are not. As demonstrated in
Chapter I, regardless of divergent views on profitability
and viability, the consensus holds that the very maintenance
of the slave system depended on the acquisition of new lands.

The geographic expansion of slavery was thought to be vital
to the health of the southern economy.

In the old economic history this view, while pos-
sessing many variations, owes its main outline to J.E.
Cairnes. Expressing northern fears of the South as a land-
swallowing predator, Cairnes argued that the very existence
of the South was tied to new land. He reasoned that wasteful
farming methods led to soil exhaustion which, in turn, man-
dated a continuous supply of fresh and fertile land. In
fact, Cairnes thought an end to expansion spelled an end to
the slave system. For without new, rich land there would be
a decrease in cotton production along with the natural increase
in the slave population. More slaves but less productive land
would cause a drop in slave prices, so that eventually,
Cairnes argued, the cost of maintaining a slave would exceed
the return on that slave's labor. The result, said Cairnes,
would be a "catastrophe."[1]

Essentially, Cairnes' argument was that slave prices
depended on territorial expansion because slave productivity
was based on the availability of new, fertile cotton lands.
This notion, with variations, appears again and again in the
writing of historians. Charles Sydnor, for example, believed
that the very fortunes of the South were bound firmly to the

---

[1] J.E. Cairnes, The Slave Power, 269.

demand for slave labor prompted by territorial expansion.[2]
So, too, Eugene Genovese's view that the South was lurching
toward a general crisis pivots on a ruinous necessity for
the newer South to maintain its demand for slaves from the
old South.[3]

Not all explanations of southern land hunger are
so explicit -- some are merely assumed to be self-evident.
Less precise but no less insistent "facts" are offered by
almost every investigator of the antebellum South. For
instance, Barrington Moore said simply: "Fresh virgin lands
were necessary for the best profits."[4] More obscurely, a
recent Ph.D. dissertation in this field proclaimed: "An
expanding slave economy supported a growing slaveholding
class whose needs were met by a politics which demanded the
right to more slave territory."[5] Like Cairnes' argument on
slave prices, these and other explanations are based on the
idea that southern agricultural methods exhausted the soil
(thereby reducing both the size of the cotton crop and
planters' income) so that the movement toward fresh, fertile
soil was economically irresistible. It follows that those

[2] Sydnor, Slavery in Miss., 202.

[3] Genovese, Political Economy, 144.

[4] Barrington Moore, Social Origins of Dictatorship
and Democracy (Boston: Beacon Press, 1966) 132.

[5] William Barney, "Road to Revolution: the Social
Basis of Secession in Alabama and Mississippi," unpublished
Ph.D. dissertation, Columbia, 1971, 443.

who remained behind working inferior soil engaged in rearing slaves for sale in the newer South in order to shore up their incomes.

Ironically, two giants of antebellum history did not believe that land was a life-giving tonic. Ulrich B. Phillips emphasized the pull of wanderlust rather than the push of soil exhaustion as a primary factor in westward migration. In fact, Phillips thought that land expansion had already been too rapid for the health of the Southern economy.[6] Charles Ramsdell argued the South had grown too large and that subsequent overproduction of cotton would drive down both the price of cotton and slaves.[7] Yet Phillips and Ramsdell were virtually alone in their views.

New economic historians, as well, echo the mainstream opinion of land expansion. Alfred Conrad and John Meyer repeated, albeit in technical terms, the argument that profits for the old South depended on the extension of slavery into the new South. They argued that without the continued demand for slaves in the cotton belt, returns to slavebreeding in the poorer regions of the old South would have fallen below the rate necessary to keep plantation profits competitive with alternative investments.[8] Richard Sutch and James Foust

---

[6] Phillips, _American Negro_, 169-186, 399.

[7] Ramsdell, "Natural Limits," 169-171.

[8] Conrad and Meyer, "The Economics," 360.

and Dale Swan, in studies on the workings of the slave
market vis-a-vis regional differences in rates of return,
also found that the demand for slaves in the new South
kept up rates of return in the old South.[9] These historians were not theorizing in a total vacuum. Important
southerners had spoken of the need to expand and it is
well known that southerners eyed with relish Mexico, Cuba,
South America and even the Pacific coast both before and
during the Civil War.[10]

For all its longevity and popularity, the argument that new land underwrote the economic health of the
South has never been fully investigated. While the argument
itself is a monument that almost everybody believes to be

[9] Sutch, "Profitability Revisited," 377; Foust
and Swan, "Productivity," 58. Some writers have confused
the territorial expansion argument with the need for free
flows of slaves between East and West within the South.
Such movements were necessary to equalize slave productivity in all regions of the South. Indeed, slave prices
would have dropped in South Carolina if a wall had been
erected around the state in 1850. This is not to say, however, that it was in the general interest of the South
that the cotton growing lands themselves expand. This confusion is, in fact, an irrelevant diversion from the historical issues, since no hindrance to East-West exchange of
slaves was ever contemplated.

[10] Robert F. Durden, "J.D.B. DeBow: Convolutions
of a Slavery Expansionist," Journal of Southern History
XVII, (November, 1951) 441-461; Percy Lee Rainwater,
"Economic Benefits of Secession: Opinions in Mississippi
in the 1850's" JSH I (November, 1935) 459; W. H. Watford,
"Confederate Western Ambitions," Southwestern Historical
Quarterly XLIV (October, 1940), 161-187; J. Fred Rippey,
"Mexican Projects of the Confederacy," SHQ (April,
1919) 241-317.

built on a firm foundation, few have actually inspected
the support pillars. Knowing that a market for slaves
existed in the South -- that slaves born in the old South
worked the soil of the new South -- is surely different
from knowing what effect land expansion had on the southern
economy. The presumption that the impact was beneficial,
even necessary in the sense that rates of return on slave
ownership were maintained throughout the South, is the same
as presuming the monument has a strong foundation. For,
the assertion that slave prices depended on the demand for
slaves is only a description of the visible part of the
monument. On what, it might be asked, does the demand for
slaves depend?

The answer suggested by economic theory is that the
demand for slaves depended on the marginal physical productivity of slaves (the output of the last slave employed)
and on the price of their output, cotton. On the more fertile
lands of the new South, the amount of cotton produced by a
slave on an acre was higher than on the thin soils of the old
South.[11] But higher slave productivity meant more output,
or an increase in the supply of cotton. Since the demand
curve for cotton sloped downward, more cotton meant lower

----

[11] For a discussion of slave productivity
between east and west, see Conrad and Meyer, "Slavery in
the Ante-Bellum South," 348.

cotton prices.

Thus, land expansion was potentially a two-edged
sword. Every increase in land for cotton production carried
with it two effects -- an increase in marginal physical
productivity of slaves and an increase in the supply of
cotton. An increase in marginal physical productivity made
slaves more valuable, but an increase in the supply of cotton
drove down the price of cotton and tended to depress the
value of slaves. Hence, it is not sufficient to link
slave values to the demand for slaves. The very reason for
that demand which raised slave values -- increased slave
physical productivity on fertile soil -- also carried with
it the possibility of lowered slave values through reduced
cotton prices. Hence the effect of land expansion on slave
values is neither obvious nor simple.

The first new economic historian to acknowledge
some of the possible paradoxes in land expansion was Peter
Passell. In an article analyzing the marginal effect of
antebellum public land sales in the South on national income,
Passell found that an increase in acreage would not have
increased national income. Quite the contrary, the net
impact would have been negative. Passell concluded that two
million additional acres in 1835 would have added 13.6
million dollars present value to the domestic cotton textile
industry through increased output. However, the loss in
export receipts (cotton sales) of 37.3 million dollars due

to a drop in the price of cotton through increased output, would have meant a net loss of 23.7 million dollars.[12]

Passell advanced both figures and conclusions cautiously, but a later work by Passell and Gavin Wright more firmly described the paradoxes of land expansion. In this study, Passell and Wright analyzed the impact of a hypothetical land increase on the price of slaves. They theorized that the value of a slave equals the price of cotton times the marginal physical product of slaves minus annual maintenance costs, all divided by the discount rate for slave assets. This equation follows from capital theory: the value of an asset equals the dicounted value of the net income generated by the asset. Using this equation, Passell and Wright estimated the effect which a hypothetical 10% increase in cotton land, made in 1830, would have had on the value of slaves. As discussed above, any increase in the supply of cotton land would increase the supply of cotton but decrease the price of cotton; simultaneously, an in-

---

[12] Peter Passell, "The Impact of Cotton Land Distribution on the Antebellum Economy," JEH XXI (December, 1971) 924-939. The possible income streams and the 1835 present value of income generated by the sale of an additional 2 million acres of cotton land are: (1) total product of the domestic cotton textile industry, without depletion -- 13.6 million dollars, with depletion -- 6.1 million dollars; (2) export receipts from lost cotton sales, without depletion -- -37.3 million, with depletion -- -16.5 million dollars; (3) opportunity cost of labor attracted to cotton agriculture, with depletion -- -21.6 million dollars.

crease of cotton land would increase the marginal physical product of slaves. Since both these components -- the price of cotton and the marginal physical product of slaves -- help determine the value of slaves, the net result will indicate in which direction land expansion affected the value of slaves. Passell and Wright found that: ". . . the fall in the price of cotton exceeds the increase in labor productivity; the net impact of land expansion on the value of a slave appears to be negative."[13] Thus, at the margin, territorial expansion tended to have an adverse effect on the value of slaves.

These two studies of the antebellum economy point in quite a different direction from that of mainstream opinion. Indeed, here are two statements about the impact of additional land on the slave economy which contradict most of what has been assumed to be true. Rather than being an economic necessity, it appears that territorial expansion had some unfortunate effects. The work of Passell and Wright so strongly suggests the need for a reinterpretation of the land question that a thorough examination is long overdue.

This thesis will attempt such an examination. First, we will present a more complex and exact analysis of the impact of expansion on the antebellum southern economy; second, we will apply those findings to the politics of expansion in

---

[13] Peter Passell and Gavin Wright, "The Effects of Pre-Civil Territorial Expansion on the Price of Slaves," JPE (November-December, 1972) 1193.

order to gain insight into southern political behavior.

Economic analysis has undoubtedly made a valuable
contribution in telling us that land expansion had a negative
impact on national income, slave values and so on. This
general observation about the economic effects of land expansion will, however, immediately bring questions to the
mind of the historian: whose interests were served? Not
served? Who suffered the least? The most? How much was
won? Lost? What were the politics? When? Where, exactly?
In dealing with the South, particularly, an aggregate picture
has only limited use -- the South was far from a monolithic
chunk of interests, its economic political goals were not
entirely homogeneous.

Thus it will be the first task of this thesis to
judge the impact of land expansion in terms of the historian's
queries. We shall want to know precisely how land movement
affected the distribution of southern wealth, i.e., the value
of slaves and of existing land. We shall ask about the
holders of that wealth: who were the gainers and losers
from expansion, and by how much? We will attack the problem
not only from the standpoint of theory, but empirically as
well, in an effort to answer those questions.

                *   *   *   *   *   *

Most obviously, the South was both "older" and

"newer." Like the North, the South was westward moving.
The end of the War of 1812 triggered a westward drift;
people pushed into the Mississippi Territory and Alabama,
Kentucky and Tennessee. By 1815 a "newer" South of Kentucky, Tennessee, Alabama, Mississippi and Louisana had
begun to distinguish itself from the older South of Maryland,
Virginia, North and South Carolina, and Georgia. An by 1830,
an even newer South was taking shape -- the state of Arkansas was added to Alabama, Mississippi and Louisiana. By
1845 Texas and Florida, too, could be included in the bur-
geoning new South. The distinction between old and new
South corresponded roughly to eastern and western South.
This fulcrum is different than that between upper and lower
South, which depended on crops. The upper South -- Maryland,
Virginia, North Carolina, Kentucky and Tennessee -- produced
tobacco and grains. The lower South, on the other hand,
could count sugar and rice among its cash crops.

Although the South as a whole had an economy best
characterized by its cotton produced by slave labor, this
feature received different emphasis in different sections.
For, the cotton economy was a complicated entity. As the
following brief history will show, the southern economy was
a dynamic system with several key aspects all changing in
relation to one another.

The antebellum South could be defined by cotton.
All the states participated in the cotton economy; cotton

shaped the South's market economy. During the 45 years
between 1815 and the eve of the Civil War, cotton production
increased from almost 209,000 bales to well over four and
one-half million bales.[14] In this same period, more than
half the total value of U.S. domestic exports was made up
of cotton.[15] Clearly, cotton represented a vital chunk
of the national economy as well as the southern economy.

But it hadn't always been so. In fact, before the
1790's cotton had only a minor role in the economy. The
classic account of the introduction of sea island cotton
indicates how little considered cotton was: in 1786,
three large bags of cotton seed arrived in Georgia, a gift
for Frank Levitt. Apparently the gift was only partially
satisfactory; Mr. Levitt tossed the seeds out on a dunghill so that he might rather use the bags. In the spring,
as the story goes, Levitt, discovering that the seeds had
sprouted, transplanted them and began cultivation. Mr.
Levitt's dunghill thus began to change the face of the
southern economy.

Sea island, or long staple, cotton could not be
successfully cultivated inland however; and the short staple
cotton which could grow almost anywhere was extremely dif-

---

[14] Paul Gates, The Farmer's Age: Agriculture 1815-
1860 (New York: Holt, Rhinehart & Winston, 1960) 145. One
bale was equal to 400 pounds of cotton.

[15] Stuart Bruchey, Cotton and the Growth of the
American Economy 1790-1860 (New York: Harcourt, Brace &
World, 1967) 2.

ficult to clean with the simple roller gin then in use.
The next important step came four years later when Eli
Whitney invented his cotton gin.

But cultivatable cotton seed and a device to gin
it only insured a possible supply of cotton; a demand for
that cotton was just as necessary. In this case, that
demand was supplied by the Industrial Revolution and the
quickening pace of cotton textile production in England --
by 1815, cotton had become the most important export of
the United States. In fact, "(B)etween 1790 and 1815 the
new demand for cotton led to a sixtyfold increase in its
production, from 3,135 to 208,986 bales. Supply did not
catch up with demand for many years, and the price remained well above ten cents a pound . . . "[16] And, so
around the turn of the century, cotton was well on its way
to becoming King.

At first, cotton cultivation clung to the South
Carolina and Georgia coast. It gradually crept inland
covering those two states; by 1820, their production constituted more than half the total crop.[17] The 1830's,
a decade of dizzing growth and land speculation, saw cotton
engulf Alabama, Mississippi, and part of Louisiana. And

---

[16] Gates, Farmer's, 8.

[17] Bruchey, Cotton, 80.

by 1840, the outline of the Cotton Kingdom -- save Texas
-- had been drawn; eager cotton growers continued to pour
in, fleshing it out. Texas' turn began in 1850, when
people suffering from "Texas fever" started pushing in.

Most certainly, part of the westward push lay in
the lure of higher yield virgin land. Land intensive
methods employed by most planters, not an unreasonable
response to cheap land and expensive labor, did result in
loss of natural soil fertility. The loss in fertility
associated with cotton cultivation was due to water and
wind erosion (not chemical depletion as was true in tobacco cultivation). Paul Gates neatly described the ruinous method known as "clean cultivation:"

> The common practice was to plow up and down
> on the slopes and to plant cotton or corn
> in successive years without using clover
> or peas to plow under and restore humus to
> the soil. Clean cultivation of the row
> crops contributed to the destruction of
> humus and reduced the capacity of the
> land to absorb moisture; the infinites-
> imal drainage channels became clogged by
> hard-pack soil, the heavy spring and
> summer rains, not being absorbed, ran down
> the slopes and carried off the topsoil in
> suspension. Sheet erosion was not at first
> apparent save in declining yields, but when
> little gullies began to appear and to deep-
> en to the point where they were beyond
> control, abandonment of the fields was
> necessary.[18]

---

[18] Gates, Farmer's, 142. See also Passell,
"Impact," appendix, 933-937.

Just as the existence of cheap land encouraged "wasteful"
methods of cultivation, cheap land rationalized the moving on to new land rather than resuscitating the old.

Of course, the second key element in the southern
economy, in tandem with cotton, was slaves. The successful introduction of cotton, particularly the short staple
variety, insured the expansion of the slave system; for
picking cotton, and incredibly arduous task, slave labor
could be forced to work where free persons would not. The
cultivation of cotton, of course, did more than just insure
slavery: it spread slavery throughout the South. As
surely as canals and railroads opened the Midwest to family
farming, cotton was the agent of dispersion for slave
labor in the South.

The westward movement of cotton cultivation which
was mirrored by a similar movement of the slave population
is described by Lewis C. Gray:

> One of the most striking phases of the
> expansion of southern agriculture was the
> shift of slave population from the older
> planting regions -- particularly the
> border States -- to the newer planting
> regions in the lower South . . . in the
> decade 1820-1830 the selling States in-
> cluded Virginia, Maryland, Delaware,
> North Carolina, Kentucky and the District
> of Columbia. It is assumed that the
> buying Stated included South Carolina,
> Georgia, Alabama, Mississippi, Tennessee
> and Missouri, with Florida added after
> 1830 and Texas after 1850, while South

Carolina and Missouri were transferred to
the selling group.[19]

These shifts were not small relocations either. "There
is," Gray concluded, "abundant evidence that the domestic
slave trade came to be of considerable magnitude."[20]

The third element in the southern economy was
land, empty land. States established before the Louisiana
Purchase had ceded land to the federal government to be
sold as public lands; notably Virginia ceded 253,054.5
square miles in 1784.[21] Even after the focus of the
cotton economy began to shift farther and farther west,
there remained uncultivated and salable land in the old
South. In fact, as Paul Gates observed: "Declining fertility and the abandonment of fields did not mean that
the Piedmont of Georgia and South Carolina was through as
a major cotton producing area. There was still much land
that had not been cleared, and on long-used land it was
possible to restore the fertility of the soil . . . In the
fifties the amount of land in cultivation in these two
states was increased by 20% over that of the previous decade,

[19] Gray, Agriculture, 651.

[20] Gray, Agriculture, 658. See also Gates,
Farmer's, 155.

[21] Benjamin Horace Hibbard, A History of the
Public Land Policies (Madison and Milwaukee: University
of Wisconsin Press, 1965) 13.

while the amount of cotton produced increased by 31%.[22]

The largest bloc of empty land, however, belonged
to the five public land states of Alabama, Arkansas, Florida, Louisiana, and Mississippi. Texas, too, while re-
taining control over its public lands, had almost an
entire state of land to sell. In sum, during the five
decades preceding the Civil War, the South was land rich.
Indeed, some believed that the only limit in expanding
cotton cultivation was that of labor shortage: "the amount
of land to be put into cotton was restricted by the
capacity to pick."[23]

The South, hence, was divided by the same economic
elements which united it. While the whole South possessed
slaves and land, parts of the South were richer in one of
these factors than they were in the other. As some regions
lost hegemony in cotton and highly productive land, they
became relatively richer in slaves. And as other regions
gained in cotton and in land, the percentage of assets
they held as slaves declined relatively. The prices of
cotton, slaves and land were dependent on one another. But
while land expansion changed the productivity of slaves and
land, and changed the unit value of their output, cotton,

[22] Gates, Farmer's, 143.

[23] Gates, Farmer's, 137.

the westward shift affected the two factors differently.
Consequently each part of the South was affected differently, depending in which factor a particular part was
rich. Thus, we can now ask how changes in the quantity
of land affected the distribution of southern wealth.

*   *   *   *   *

Wealth in the antebellum South was mainly made
up of two kinds of property or assets -- land and slaves.[24]
We shall ask what happened to the value of existing property when new public lands were planted in cotton. In
other words, what effect did land expansion have on (a)
the value of slaves and (b) the value of land?

This dissertation will explore the counterfactual
proposition to the traditional proposition that the South
needed a diet of new land; we will ask what would have
happened to southern wealth if 10% less land had been cultivated in the South between 1840 and 1860. For, to know
what would have happened in the absence of land expansion
is to know, too, how important actual expansion was for the
southern economy. We selected 10% for expositional purposes because it is a measure which will permit us to observe

---

[24] L. Rose, "Capital Losses of Southern Slaveowners Due to Emancipation," Western Economic Journal,
3, Fall, 1964,

the direction and size of the impact of land contraction
for marginal change. The land under cultivation in the
South roughly doubled between 1840 and 1860. It is plausible that hostile federal legislators could have prevented
a portion of this new land from entering the cotton economy.
Hence, when we speak of a 10% reduction in the quantity of
land, we are speaking of a real political alternative
faced by antebellum congressmen.

Economists theorize that in a competitive economy
the market value of a productive asset -- a slave or an
acre of land -- equals the discounted value of the income
stream generated by the asset:

$$V = \frac{R_1}{(1+i)} + \frac{R_2}{(1+i)^2} + \frac{R_3}{(1+i)^3} \ldots \ldots \frac{R_n}{(1+i)^n} \tag{1}$$

where V = value of the asset

       R_n = the income produced by the asset in the nth year

       i = the annual rate of discount

If one assumes that the income each year is approximately the same, that the discount rate used is the same
for year year, and that the income will continue to flow
"forever," the formula can be simplified to the following:

$$V = \frac{R}{i} \tag{2}$$

where R = one year's income

Marginal productivity distribution theory[25] suggests
that the annual income from a slave or an acre of land
equals the value of the marginal product less any maintenance costs. For slaves, the value of the marginal product
equals the marginal physical product -- the extra cotton
produced by having the last slave in the fields -- times
the revenue per unit of cotton:

$$(VMP_{slave} = MPP_{slave} \cdot Price_{cotton}).$$

But slaves must be fed, housed and clothed, so the net
revenue from owning a slave can be written:

(3)

$$Net\ Revenue_{slave} = MPP_{slave} \cdot Price_{cotton} - Maintenance$$

Similarly, the formula for land is:

$$Revenue_{land} = MPP_{land} \cdot Price_{cotton} \qquad (4)$$

Substituting into the asset value formula:

$$V_{slave} = \frac{MPP_{slave} \cdot Price_{cotton} - Maintenance}{i} \qquad (5)$$

$$V_{land} = \frac{MMP_{land} \cdot Price_{cotton}}{i} \qquad (6)$$

---

[25] Paul Samuelson, Economics 8th Edition (New York:
McGraw-Hill Bk Co. 1970) 519-521.

Hence, to find out what will happen to the value
of either asset we analyze changes to the marginal physical products, to the price of cotton and the the discount
rate. The equations can be rewritten in rates-of-change
form as:

$$V_{slave}{}^* = K(MPP_{slave}{}^* + Price_{cotton}{}^*) - i^* \tag{7}$$

$$V_{land}{}^* = MMP_{land}{}^* + Price_{cotton}{}^* - i^* \tag{8}$$

where * refers to percentage change
$$K = a \ constant^{26}$$

Since we assume land expansion will not influence the discount
rate, $i^* = 0$ for all our cases, so the formula becomes:

$$V_{slave}{}^* = K(MMP_{slave}{}^* + Price_{cotton}{}^*) \tag{9}$$

$$V_{land}{}^* = MMP_{land}{}^* + Price_{cotton}{}^* \tag{10}$$

In other words, the change in the value of an asset depends
upon the change in its MMP and the price of its output.

Bearing in mind the asset value formula, we suggest
the economics of westward expansion can be understood

---

[26] Fogel and Engerman Reinterpretation, 339. The
constant "K" allows for the averaging effects of the fixed
maintenance costs in the rate-of-change formula.

through two scenarios. Two scenarios are necessary because perceived economic interests are not always identical
to real economic interest, a divergence which may be particularly relevant in this case. In the first scenario,
the one perceived by southerners, only the value of the
MMP's are affected. The price of cotton is unaffected; i.e.,
the demand for cotton is thought to be perfectly elastic
with respect to price. This is a plausible assumption since,
in a competitive system, producers perceive the demand curve
facing them to be perfectly elastic. Under this scenario,
the MMP of slaves decreases because 10% less land meant
less land for them to work. This can be shown in Figure
1. The marginal physical product of slave labor (MPP_s) in
cotton production is shown by xy on the graph. If there are
Q slaves, the MPP_s or marginal output of the last slave is
C. When land is subtracted from the cotton economy, slave
labor becomes less productive and the MPP_s schedule shifts
downward to x'y'. Now the MPP of the Qth slave falls to C'.
And since the value of a slave varies with its productivity,
slave value will also go down.

Similarly, a decrease in land will increase the MMP
of existing land. In Figure II, the marginal output of the
L^{th} acre of land is A. Less land "concentrates" the labor
force, so with L' acres in production the MPP of land rises
to A'. Hence, the value of a unit of land would tend to
rise under a decrease in land.

FIGURE I

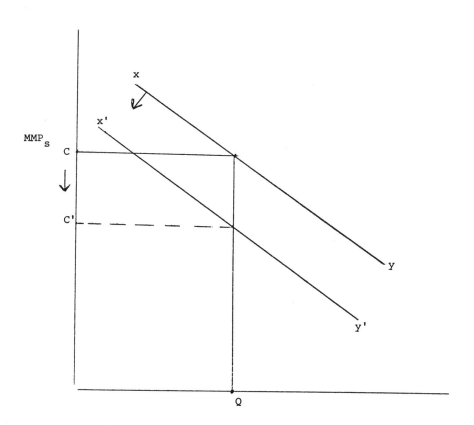

Quantity of Slaves

FIGURE II

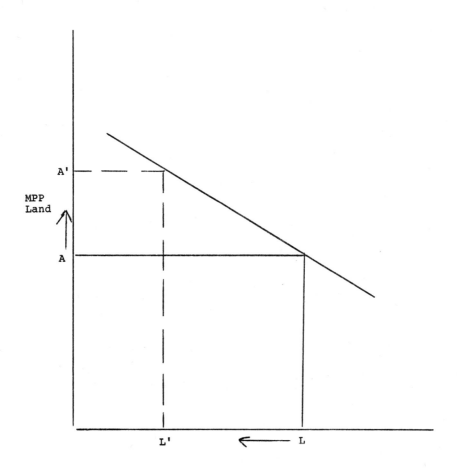

Quantity of Land

Under scenario 1, then, slowed westward expansion
has a negative impact on the value of a slave and a positive impact on the value of land so that sections of the
South holding most of their wealth in slaves lose from the
hypothetical decrease in land while sections rich in land
gain.

Consider, however, a second scenario, one which was
presumably not understood by southerners and one which
would make gainers of all sections. The first scenario
assumes that land contraction would have had no impact on
the price of cotton. This assumption is illustrated in
Figure III. As the supply curve, S, shifts inward with a
land contraction to S', the equilibrium price of cotton
remains at P. But if the demand curve for cotton was not
perfectly elastic, which in fact it was not, then cotton
prices must rise as supply shifts to the left as shown in
Figure IV. A reduction in land, given that the demand curve
was not perfectly elastic, would have been beneficial to all
sections because the price of cotton would have gone up.

Hence, in our second scenario, the one which reflects
economic reality, along with the effect a land contraction
had on (a) the MPP of slaves and (b) the MPP of land, we
need to have a measure of its impact on a third factor (c)
the price of cotton, in order to calculate what would happen
to the value of slaves and land.

Estimates of the percentage change in the MPP_s of

FIGURE III

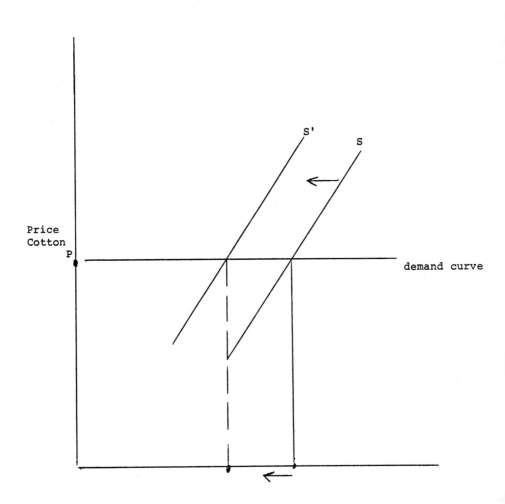

Quantity of Cotton

FIGURE IV

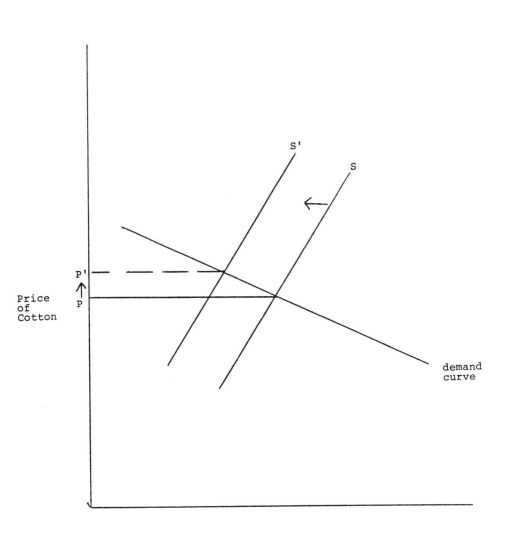

Quantity of Cotton

land and slaves and the price of cotton associated with a
given change in the quantity of land can be derived from
the work of Passell and Wright and from simple assumptions
about the productive process.

(a) MMP of slaves: the agricultural production
process -- or production function -- might reasonably be
expected to take the mathematical form known as Cobb-
Douglas.[27] Passell and Wright show that under these cir-
cumstances the elasticity of the MPP_{slave} with respect to
the quantity of land equals the percentage distribution
share of land in the output.[28]

$$\frac{MPP_{slave}^{*}}{L^{*}} = a \qquad\qquad (11)$$

where   a = land's distribution share in output

Or, multiplying both sides by L^{*}:

$$MPP_{slave}^{*} = aL^{*} \qquad\qquad (12)$$

In other words, an X% change in land changes the MPP_{slave}

---

[27] Fogel and Engerman, Reinterpretation, 338.
The mathematical form of the Cobb-Douglas production
function is $Y = AK^{a}L^{b}T^{c}$ (a+b+c = 1) where Y = output,
A = the technology constant, K = capital, L = labor,
T = land. This form is frequently assumed by economists,
both because it fits certain observed properties of production relationships and because it is mathematically
very easy to work with.

[28] Passell and Wright, "Slave Prices" JPE, 1192.

by aX%.

(b) MMP of land: The Cobb-Douglas relationship makes it equally simple to calculate the relationship between L^* and MPP_{land}^*. From the properties of the Cobb-Douglas function, we know that:

$$cotton^* = aL^* \qquad (13)$$

In other words, a percentage change in land, L^*, changes total cotton production by aL^*. The Cobb-Douglas also tells us that the distribution shares of land and slaves must remain constant percentages. So that if total cotton output goes down by aL^*, the total return to land must also go down by aL^*. However, there are L^* units less land which must divide up the cotton output, which is down by aL^*. Marginal productivity theory tells us that the per unit return to land is the same as the MPP_{land}. Hence, we can infer that:

$$MPP_{land}^* = aL^* - L^* \qquad (14)$$

$$MPP_{land}^* = (a-1) L^* \qquad (15)$$

(c) the price of cotton: The impact of a change in the quantity of land on the price of cotton is equally easy to calculate. By definition:[29]

---

[29] Samuelson, _Economics_, 361-364.

$$\text{Price}_{\text{cotton}}^* = \frac{1}{E_D} \text{ cotton}^* \qquad (16)$$

where E_D = the elasticity of demand with respect to the price of cotton. We know from Cobb-Douglas that:

$$\text{Cotton}^* = aL^* \qquad (17)$$

Substituting, we find that

$$\text{Price}_{\text{cotton}}^* = \frac{1}{E_D} aL^* \qquad (18)$$

$$\text{Price}_{\text{cotton}}^* = \frac{a}{E_D} L^* \qquad (19)$$

In other words, a change in land, L^*, will change output by aL^* which will mean a change in cotton price of $\frac{a}{E_D} L*$.

Thus, to calculate our three variables -- $\text{MPP}_{\text{slave}}^*$, $\text{MPP}_{\text{land}}^*$ and $\text{Price}_{\text{cotton}}$ -- all we need to have are estimates of "a", the distribution share of land in output, and "E_D", the price elasticity of the demand for cotton. Fogel and Engerman estimate that a = .32[30]. We take from Wright an estimate of the elasticity of demand E_D = -.65.[31] Hence, plugging in the numbers for a 10% decrease in land:

$$\text{MMP}_{\text{slave}}^* = (.32)(-10) = -3.2\% \qquad (20)$$

---

[30] Fogel and Engerman, <u>Reinterpretation</u>, 315.

[31] Gavin Wright, "An Econometric Study of Cotton Production and Trade 1830-1860," <u>The Review of Economics and Statistics</u>, LIII, (May 1971) 119.

$$MPP_{land}^* = (.32 - 1.0) \ (-10) = 6.8\% \qquad (21)$$

$$Price_{cotton} = (\frac{.32}{-.65}) \ (-10) = 4.9\% \qquad (22)$$

With these numbers in hand, we can go back to the original formulas:

for slaves

$$V_S^* = K(MMP_S^* + P_C^*) \qquad (23)$$

for land:

$$V_L^* = MPP_L^* + P_C^* \qquad (24)$$

Under the first scenario, which assumes that the price of cotton was perfectly elastic (or, $P_C^* = 0$) -- the scenario we presume southerners perceived or our "perception scenario" -- we substitute the numbers in and find that:

$$V_S^* = 1.1 \ (-3.2 + 0) = -3.52\%^{[32]} \qquad (25)$$

$$V_L^* = 6.8 + 0 = 6.8\% \qquad (26)$$

And under scenario two, which is the "reality scenario" where the demand for cotton is not perfectly elastic (or, $P_C^* = 4.9$), we find that:

---

[32] The value of the constant = 1.1. Fogel and Engerman, Reinterpretation, 339.

$$V_S^* = 1.] \ (-3.2 + 4.9) = 1.87\% \tag{27}$$

$$V_L^* = 6.8 + 4.9 = 11.7\% \tag{28}$$

Essentially, these last results mean that for a 10% decrease
in the amount of land, (a) the value of a slave would have
declined either -3.52% or risen 1,87% depending on the
elasticity of the price of cotton; (b) the value of an acre
of land would have increased by 6.8% or 11.7%, once again,
depending on which scenario one is viewing.[33] We can see
simply by glancing at equations (25) and (26) that the net
impact of a 10% land reduction will depend on the relative
size of each of the assets held: the impact on slave
wealth would have been negative and the impact on land
wealth would have been positive, so that the ultimate direction would depend on how much relative slave and land wealth
was held. Thus, the net impact under the assumptions of
scenario 1, the perception scenario, is not immediately
apparent. However, the net impact under the assumptions of
scenario 2, the reality scenario, is immediately apparent.

---

[33] Note that this relationship holds only in the
"short run"; in equilibrium, the price of a slave must
equal the cost of reproducing a slave. For our purposes,
however, it is the short run which is relevant. Even if
slaveholders could adjust their behavior to changes in
the value of slaves, the time it would take for the market
to reach equilibrium would be measured in decades. I am
grateful to Donald Dewey for this point.

Equations (27) and (28) both show positive numbers for $V_s{}^*$
and $V_L{}^*$, indicating that the impact on total wealth would
have been positive.

Thus we have solved the theoretical problem about
the direction and size of the impact of a land reduction.
Before these measurement techniques could be used, however,
other data were necessary. For, in order to find out how
the southern economy would have been affected by a reduction in land, some measures of how much wealth the South
actually had in slaves and land was required. In other
words, estimates of land and slave values, in dollar terms,
over the period 1840-1860 were necessary.

To estimate slave wealth, the number of slaves was,
of course, essential. For that, the Population Schedule of
the U.S. Census for 1850 and 1860[34] provided a county-by-county
breakdown of slaves by age and sex. But simple aggregation
was obviously inadequate. Clearly some slaves were worth
more than others; a 21 year old male in the new South had a
higher market value than a 65 year old female in the old
South. Thus, four general divisions were employed -- male,
female, old South and new South. (The old South included
Virginia, North Carolina, South Carolina, Georgia, and the
new South included Alabama, Arkansas, Florida, Mississippi,

---

[34] U.S. Bureau of the Census, Population, Washington D.C. 1850. U.S. Bureau of the Census, Population,
Washington D.C. 1860.

Louisiana, Texas and Tennessee.)[35]   Within each of these

four big divisions, a price scale based on age was esti-

mated for 1850 and for 1860.[36]   It was important to use

both Census years because the price of slaves increased

realtive to the price of land between 1850 and 1860.   Thus,

1850 prices were a reasonably accurate reflection of the

period 1840-1850, and 1860 prices were more reasonably

accurate for the decade of the 1850's.

The results of this estimate of price scales for

male-female, old-new South, for 1850 and 1860, can be seen

in Tables I through IV.   A glance at these Tables show the

variation among divisions -- from $30 for a 60-69 year old

female slave in the old South, to $1103 for a 20-29 year

old male slave in the new South;   or, in the same age and

sex category, a 20-29 year old male in the new South was

worth $200 more than his counterpart in the old South.

Using these four price scales and the assumption

that age and sex ratios varied more from state to state

than among counties within a state, an average male and

female slave price for each state was calculated for 1850

and 1860.   These average prices were obtained by sampling

at least 10% of the total counties in each state; for each

[35]   The states of Maryland and Kentucky are not
included because they participated little in the cotton
economy and did not fight on the Confederate side during
the Civil War.

[36]   Based on figures from William Fogel and Stanley
Engerman, Time on the Cross, vol. I, 72-76; vol. II, 79-86.

TABLE   I

Male Slave Prices in 1850, in Current Dollars

Ages	Old South Price	New South Price
0 - 4	100	140
5 - 9	325	453
10 - 14	540	754
15 - 19	680	950
20 - 29	790	1103
30 - 39	730	1019
40 - 49	525	733
50 - 59	290	405
60 - 69	100	140

Source: See text.

TABLE II

Female Slave Prices in 1850, in Current Dollars

Ages	Old South Price	New South Price
0 - 4	100	140
5 - 9	325	453
10 - 14	485	678
15 - 19	590	825
20 - 29	630	880
30 - 39	515	719
40 - 49	330	461
50 - 59	145	202
60 - 69	30	42

Source: See text.

TABLE III

Male Slave Prices in 1860, in Current Dollars

Ages	Old South Price	New South Price
0 - 4	203	229
5 - 9	658	740
10 - 14	1232	1231
15- 19	1378	1550
20 - 29	1600	1800
30 - 39	1478	1663
40 - 49	1064	1197
50 - 59	587	661
60 - 69	203	229

Source: See text.

TABLE IV

<u>Female Slave Prices in 1860, in Current Dollars</u>

<u>Ages</u>	<u>Old South Price</u>	<u>New South Price</u>
0 - 4	203	229
5 - 9	6 58	740
10 - 14	983	1105
15 - 19	1196	1345
20 - 29	1276	1435
30 - 39	1042	1172
40 - 49	541	752
50 - 59	293	330
60 - 69	61	69

Source: See text.

of the sample counties, the number of slaves in each category
-- male-female, old-new South -- was multiplied by the price
for that particular age category. For example, in 1850,
Appling County, Georgia, had 450 male slaves under four years
old; a figure which, when multiplied by the price of male
slaves under four years old in the old South ($100) yields
$45,000. From the exact male and female figures from the
sample counties, an average price for male and female
slaves for each state was calculated. Obtaining separate
average state prices was a sound idea. Tables V and VI show
that average state prices did, in fact, vary a great deal;
for instance, the average price of a male in the two new
South states of Mississippi and Florida differed by almost
$100 in 1850, indicating that age and/or sex ratios varied
from state to state.

     After an average male and female price for each
state was computed, the total number of male and female
slaves in every county of a particular state was multiplied
by the respective average prices for that particular state.
Then the total male and female figures were added together
to obtain one total figure of slave wealth for each county.
Thus, this first estimation operation yielded total slave
wealth, weighted by age, sex and section, for each county
in every state in 1850 and 1860 -- 1,685 counties in all.

     Getting estimates of land wealth was less complicated.
These measurements were obtained directly from the Agricul-

TABLE   V

Average Slave Price in 1850, in Current Dollars

State	Average Male Price	Average Female Price
Alabama	621	571
Arkansas	708	579
Florida	693	549
Georgia	485	414
Louisiana	743	586
Mississippi	736	566
North Carolina	476	394
South Carolina	482	396
Tennessee	673	550
Texas	699	583
Virginia	480	388

Source: See text.

TABLE VI

Average Slave Price in 1860, in Current Dollars

State	Average Male Price	Average Female Price
Alabama	1129	952
Arkansas	1155	936
Florida	1097	933
Georgia	1054	824
Louisiana	1134	907
Mississippi	1195	942
North Carolina	999	774
South Carolina	1028	802
Tennessee	1114	870
Texas	1163	951
Virginia	1012	783

Source: See text.

ture Schedule of the Census for 1850 and 1860.[37]   In the
Schedule for 1860, the figure for "cash-value of farms"
by county was used. However, unlike 1860, the designation
in the 1850 Census included "value of farming implements
and machinery." In order to subtract the value of farming
implements and machinery from straight cash value, a calculation was made to determine the proportion that this category constituted of combined wealth in each state ten
years later in the 1860 Census when the two categories were
separately listed. This figure, which turned out generally
to be rather small and averaged 3%, was subtracted from
each county in the 1850 Census. Thus, a figure for total
land wealth for every southern county in 1850 and 1860 was
estimated.

What all these operations yielded, then, are the
following measures: (1) the percentage change a 10% land
decrease would have had on slave and land wealth assuming
that cotton prices were perfectly elastic, the perception
scenario; (2) the percentage change a 10% land decrease
would have had on slave and land wealth assuming that cotton
prices were not perfectly elastic, the reality scenario;
(3) county-by-county estimates of actual wealth held in
slaves in the South for 1850 and 1860; (4) county-by-county
estimates of actual wealth held in land in the South for 1850
and 1860. What remained, then, was to measure the effect

a land contraction would have had on total wealth.   In
other words, we had the information necessary to answer
the question: what impact would a reduction in land have
had on actual southern wealth?

Under scenario 1, in which decreased land sales
have a negative impact on the value of slaves (-3.52%) but
a positive impact on the value of land (6.8%), we multiplied total slave wealth in each county by -.0352, and total
land wealth in each county by .068. Then we combined those
two figures to obtain the single net impact of the land
reduction. The net impact, of course, could be either
positive or negative, depending on the particular mix of
land and slave wealth in the county. For example, in 1850,
Appling County, Georgia, held $172,387 in slave wealth and
$146,434 in land wealth. A 10% reduction in land would
have meant a loss of $6,068 in slave wealth but a $9,957
gain in land wealth; Appling County, thus, is a county
which would have experienced a net gain from a land contraction -- a net impact of $3,889, to be exact.

In scenario 2, which included the less-than-perfect
price esasticity of cotton, the sign of the impact on slave
values changed from negative to positive -- from -3.52% to
+1.87% -- and the impact on land value increased from 6.8%
to 11.7%. Thus, under scenario 2, the net impact on every
county would have been positive. In Appling County, the
effect of a land contraction would have been a $3,224 gain

in slave wealth and a $17,133 gain in land wealth; or
a net impact of $20,357 gain in total wealth for 1850.[38]

The final results of these operations under the
assumptions of scenario 1, the perception scenario, are
immediately apparent by looking at Maps I and II. Under
this scenario, which assumes that cotton is indeed King
such that its demand curve is perfectly elastic, many
parts of the South would not have gained from land expansion. Instead, large areas of both the Southeast and
Southwest would have gained by a 10% reduction in land.
In 1850, Map I, the black areas representing a gain from
land contraction are exactly where we might expect: the
rich Piedmont and Alluvial areas of the Carolinas, Georgia,
Alabama, Arkansas, Mississippi and Louisiana, along with
some parts of Texas, Tennessee and Florida. These areas
were sufficiently fertile that the relative concentration
of wealth was in land rather than in slaves. Thus, these

---

[38] We worked under the assumption that almost
all land in the South was potentially cotton land -- the
notion that if the price of cotton climbed high enough,
most land would have been converted into cotton land.
However, while this might be a perfectly acceptable assumption for economic theory, we modified it for historical
purposes. In those counties that the Census showed no,
or miniscule, cotton production but high production of
tobacco, wool, meat, sugar or rice over the 1850-1860
period, we assumed that the land was not "cotton land,"
and that the price of cotton would have no effect on land
value. In those cases we used impact on land value = 0
for both scenarios. In some Virginia counties, for
example, we calculated the percentage changes in slave
values, but assumed the changes in land value to be 0.

MAP I

Pattern of Impact of 10% Land Reduction on
Southern Counties, 1850, Under Scenario I

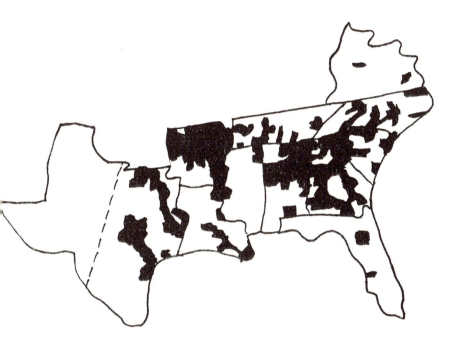

■ = gain from land reduction

☐ = loss from land reduction

land-rich areas would have gained from a reduction in land
cultivated elsewhere.

Looking at Map II, for 1860, the distribution of
losses and gains under the perception scenario which were
associated with a 10% land reduction is, again, what we
might expect. The black areas, or those parts which stood
to gain, have moved westward. The areas which are now
relatively richer in land than in slaves have their great-
est concentration in the West: although black patches
still appear in the Piedmont, the bulk of land-rich areas
lie in the Black Prairie region of Alabama and Mississippi,
the Alluvial regions of Tennessee, Arkansas, Mississippi,
Louisiana and Texas, and great poritons of Texas and Arkansas.

Maps I and II illustrate two important facts about
the antebellum economy. First, land values were moving
westward, always toward richer and more fertile areas. It
might well have been this westward shift which convinced
many southerners and historians alike that economic salva-
tion lay in land expansion. After all, this geographic
shift seemed to set up a beneficial symmetry: as land
values moved West the eastern regions became relatively richer
in slaves -- an input sorely needed on the frontiers of the
cotton economy. The Southwest, rich in land, bought slaves
from the Southeast, a region which was presumably happy to
supply them.

MAP II

Pattern of Impact from a 10% Land
Reduction on Southern Counties,
1860, Under Scenario I.

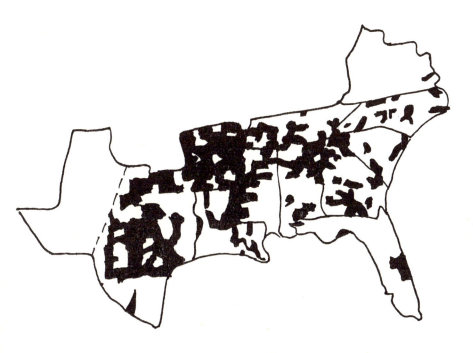

■ = gain from land reduction

☐ = loss from land reduction

But Maps I and II show that this westward drift
had a not-so-beneficial impact on land rich regions. As
land values shifted westward, those regions which were
relatively rich in land suffered net losses in total land
and slave assets. On the other hand, regions which were
relatively rich in slaves enjoyed a net gain from that
westward expansion.

Thus the two maps indicate that the South (under
Scenario 1) did not have a clear or unified financial stake
in westward expansion. Those areas which were relatively
richer in land would have gained from a slowed, or reduced,
expansion; and those richer in slaves would have lost
from such a reduction. Specifically, a cotton planter
sitting on fertile alluvial soil in Washington County,
Mississippi, would have been better off if expansion had
been halted, just as a planter in Beaufort County, South
Carolina, would have been worse off if total land in cultivation had been reduced.

But these conflicts of interest were conflicts
only under the assumptions of the perception scenario.
Scenario 1, after all, assumes that the demand for cotton
was perfectly elastic, so that increasing the supply of
cotton -- as happened when its production was expanded into
fertile western lands -- would not have reduced the price
of cotton. This, however, was not the case. We know that

the demand for cotton was not perfectly elastic. Moreover, we know that when we include demand elasticity in
the value of assets formula, the result is startling: the
value of both land and slaves would have benefitted from
a 10% reduction in land. Under the reality scenario, then,
maps of the South for 1850 and 1860 would appear solidly
black. Of course, all gains would have been relative in
that some would have gained more than others. Nonetheless,
under scenario 2, the South did in fact have a unified,
single interest in land expansion/land reduction, although
certainly not the same interest that has been presumed by
historians. In reality, whether land-rich or slave-rich,
every region in the South would have been better off if
land expansion had not proceeded apace during 1840-1860.

For the moment, let us ignore scenario 2. There
were, after all, differential gainers under that scenario:
for example, in 1850 the gains from a land reduction ranged
from 9.26% in Jackson County, Arkansas, to only 3.65% in
Carteret County, North Carolina. And in this sense scenario
2 is a less dramatic statement of scenario 1. But scenario
1 is more than drama; it is, perhaps, also the way the
South understood itself. We shall examine that picture of
economic conflict.

CHAPTER III

THE POLITICS OF WESTWARD EXPANSION

Historians frequently cast the South's economic
conflict of interest in geographical terms: the old, farmed-
out, tumbledown Southeast versus the new, rich, teeming
Southwest. The Southeast appeared to offer little competition to the Southwest whose seduction of younger sons and
slaves only compounded the economic erosion already taking
place in the Southeast. Charles Sydnor, the historian of
southern sectionalism, located the beginning of a conscious
conflict in the 1820's.[1]

This conflict began in part, and was aggravated
in part, by the seeming limitless amount of new land which
could be developed as "Southwest." By 1840 the public domain was comprised of millions and millions of acres in
Arkansas, Alabama, Mississippi, Louisiana and Florida.

This disposition of these lands fell to the U.S.
Congress. During the first several decades of the new
Republic, Congress viewed the public domain as a source of
revenue. Congressional policy favored sale at the highest
price possible and in large blocs -- creating both a speculator's paradise and a fulsome revenue-raising operation.

---

[1] For example, see Charles Sydnor, The Development
of Southern Sectionalism, (Louisiana State University Press,
1948) Chapter XI. And p.12.

Under the Act of 1796, half of the public lands were to be
put on the market in tracts of 5,760 acres, the remainder
in chunks of 640 acres. Minimum price per acre was set at
$2.00 and a credit provision of one half down, one year to
pay the rest was generally viewed as quite strict in an era
when private land mortgages were difficult to obtain. The
Act was repealed four years later by a more liberal -- but
by no means democratic -- law which reduced the amount of
acreage in salable tracts to 320 acres and extended credit
for a period of four years; the minimum price of $2.00
an acre remained. Subsequent acts reduced the price to
$1.64 an acre and allowed sale of 160 acre tracts (Act of
1804).[2]

However, the attitude toward the public domain as
a revenue source began to change in the 1820's, mostly under
pressure from settlers who were fanning out over the country,
pushing the frontiers west. These settlers, more often
squatters, began to come into conflict with wealthy land investors, and they increasingly turned to Congress for pro-
tection and relief. As the West grew in political importance,
Congress responded, and gradually a new land policy evolved.
The new land policy involved a change in primary objective:
settlement rather than revenue.

Under provisions of the Act of 1820, the minimum

[2] Roy Robbins. Our Landed Heritage (Princeton
University Press: Princeton, New Jersey. 1942) 16-17, 18,
24-25.

price per acre was further lowered to $1.25 and the minimum
amount of land which could be purchased was reduced to 80
acres. The Act, however, offered no credit provision at
all.[3] The reduction in the price and acreage favored the
settler, while the abolition of credit favored the speculator
with access to the private capital market.

But a decade later, the political triumph of the
settler was reflected in the passage of the Preemption Law
of 1830. Under this law, settlers' claims of the preceding
year (1829) to enter public land before purchase were recognized -- squatters were entitled to buy, after the fact, up
to 160 acres for the minimum price of $1.25 per acre regard-
less of the land's market value. Although the preemption
principle gave relief to those who had already entered and
often cultivated the public domain, it also encouraged
continued 'illegal' entry; the basic issue remained unre-
solved and temporary preemption was reaffirmed by Congress a
number of times until it was replaced by the Act of 1841.[4]

In 1841, Congress finally legalized the right of a
settler to enter and cultivate the public lands before
purchase, providing however that the lands had been surveyed,
although not yet offered for sale. The Preemption Act of

---

[3] Robbins, Landed, 34.

[4] Robbins, Landed, 50.

1841 made preemption open to the head of a family -- a
man over the age of 21 or a widow -- a citizen or an alien
intending to become a citizen, the maximum purchase was
not to exceed 160 acres, and was to be paid at the minimum
rate of $1.25 an acre. As a defense against speculators,
the law required that the preemptor sign an affadavit declaring that he or she did not own over 320 acres of other lands,
or abandon any other residence in the same state or territory in order to claim land under the Act.[5] This law was
renewed, in essentially the same form, over the next twenty
years.[6]

A second scheme of land distribution extant during the
antebellus period was graduation -- a device to peg the price
of lands to the number of years the parcel had been on the
market -- a sort of price slashing operation to encourage
purchase of less desirable lands. Graduation bills failed
in 1830, 1846, and 1850. In 1854, however, a law finally
passed. The Act provided that unsold lands on the market
for ten or more years could be sold at $1.00 an acre; land
on the market for 15 or more years could be sold at $.75 an
acre; 20 or more years at $.50 an acre; and 30 or more years

[5] Robbins, Landed, 89-91.

[6] Congressional Globe, 32 Congress, 2 session;
Cong. Globe, 33 Cong., 1 sess.

at 12½ cents per acre.[7]

The third distribution scheme advanced during the
antebellum period was, of course, homestead. A reversal
from the original intent fo using the public domain as a
revenue source, homestead was the notion that the public
domain should be employed solely as a means of redistri-
buting wealth and rewarding private initiative: public
lands should be free to those willing to settle and cultivate them. The homestead proposal was simply to give 160
acres of land to any head of a family, over the age of 21,
a citizen or alien intending to become a citizen, who had
resided on and cultivated the land for five years.

The first homestead bill was introduced during the
29th Congress in 1845, bu the first real debate did not
take place until five years later, in the 31st Congress.
The bill was debated and voted on without success during
the 31st, 32nd, 33rd, 35th and 36th Congresses. Finally, in
1862, the homestead bill passed into law.[8]

---

[7] Cong. Globe, 29 Cong., 1 sess., 2109, 1058, 1071,
1094, 1108, Cong. Globe, 31 Cong., 1 sess., 78, 297; 2 sess.,
720. Cong. Globe, 33 Cong., 1 sess., 169, 894, 903, 917, 918
2204.

[8] Cong. Globe, 31 cong., 1 sess., 131, 408, 423, 448,
1122, 1441, 1474; 2 sess., 22, 50, 752. Cong. Globe, 32 Cong.,
1 sess., 58, 670, 685, 707, 723, 926, 1275-1284, 1311-1320, 1351,
2194, 2267; 2 sess., 747. Cong. Globe, 33 Cong., 1 sess., 47, 419,
423, 500, 507-549, 1832, 1844, 1913. Cong. Globe, 35 Cong., 1
sess., 181, 324, 1130; 2 sess., 210, 725, 726, 1074. Cong. Globe,
36 Cong., 1 sess., 1014, 1114-1115, 2042-2043, 1750, 2221, 2222,
2420, 2988, 3178, 3262; 2 sess., 15. Cong. Globe, 37 Cong., 2
sess., 1035, 1951.

Thus, during the period 1820-1860, settlement
gradually took precedence over revenue in the congressional
mind as the West (and Southwest) began to grow in political
power. Settlement over revenue was what the West and Southwest wanted; and, for a time, the Southeast was in agreement. However, as it became apparent that the growth of the
Southwest had economic and political repercussions, settlement itself became an issue. Land distribution, its method
and hence it pace, became a question of vital importance
to the South.

At first, both sections seemed to favor a cheap
land policy, which meant rapid distribution of public lands.
Raymond Wellington, in a study on the political and sectional
influences on public lands, found that the West and South
acted together until 1832 against the Northeast and high
land prices.[9] Roy Robbins, in a similar study, also found
an alliance between the South and the West until the early
1830's. Thereafter, however, a gradual dissolution set in,
so that by 1854 the South Atlantic states even challenged
the graduation bill.[10] These findings are echoed by George
Stephenson's political history of public lands which argued
that the Southwest remained friendly to schemes to graduate

---

[9] Raymond Wellington, The Political and Sectional
Influence of the Public Lands (Riverside Press: New York, 1914)
114.

[10] Robbins, Landed, 50, 169.

the price of land and even to the free land of the homestead bills, while the Southeast was unalterably opposed.[11]
And Fred Shannon's article on the Homestead Act made the point
that the division of votes over the homestead bills in 1852
and 1853 was between the Southeast and Northeast on the one
hand, and the Southwest and Northwest on the other.[12]

Most recently, Gerald Wolff, in an article on the
homestead bill of 1854, found that the Southeast and Southwest split over homestead in 1854. Using Guttman scale
analysis, which provides a pattern of preferences on roll
calls surrounding the homestead proposals and amendments, he
argued that the South was far from united against homestead. He also tested the Robbins and Stephenson arguments
on graduation legislation and found that Guttman scalogram
substantiated their case of a split along geographic lines.[13]

We have, thus, a picture of political conflict over
the distribution of public lands. Beginning in the early
1830's, the Southeast starts to split off from its alliance
with the Southwest -- a division which remains clear through-

---

[11] George Stephenson, The Political History of Public
Lands (Richard G. Badger; Boston, 1917) 127, 114, 147. Helene
Zahler, Eastern Workingmen and National Land Policy, (Colum-
bia University Press: New York, 1941) 124, 173, 187-188.

[12] Fred Shannon, "The Homestead Act and the Labor
Surplus," AHR XVI, (July, 1936) 642.

[13] Gerald Wolff, "The Slavocracy and the Homestead
Problem of 1854," Ag. Hist. 40, (April, 1966) 101-111.

out the decade of the 1850's. This political conflict is presumed to have had an economic base; specifically, that the economic interests of the Southeast were opposed to the rapid distribution of new and competitive lands, while the Southwest was in favor of a cheap and rapid land distribution policy.

This political split is at variance with the presumption, explained earlier, that the Southeast and Southwest enjoyed a mutually beneficial economic relationship: the sale of slaves from Southeast to Southwest. It seems apparent that the political and economic definitions of sectional interests are inadequate. We know already that the economic theory behind Southeast-Southwest sectionalism yields an empirical picture far less clean than a simple geographic split. In fact, we know that while the East-West split holds up in general, the precise split is one between those sections relatively rich in land and those rich in slaves -- demarcations which fall on either side of an East-West division. Under the perception scenario, there are areas in both East and West sections which would have lost from land expansion as well as areas which would have gained from expansion.

Perhaps the same refinement may also be true of the political split. If the true economic split between sections was based on land wealth versus slave wealth, then we might expect to find that the political division followed

along these lines, too. A test of harmony between economic
and political interest involves two stages. First, we shall
test for simple correspondence. Did political differences
divide into the same geographic areas as did our economic
differences? Second, if the first test is satisfied, we
shall ask whether those political divisions reflected an
accurate assessment of economic interest. Did political
behavior act to reinforce economic interests, or did it
act against those interests?

*   *   *   *   *

In political history, one of the most obvious ways
to take the political pulse is through voting behavior.
Indeed, most of the students of land policy and politics
we spoke of earlier, went to the congressional record to
check debates and votes. Unfortunately, these studies did
not go beyond rough political distinctions between Southeast and Southwest which were based on even rougher economic
assumptions.

We are, however, in a position to check the correspondence between economics and politics because we have
economic wealth data on a county-by-county basis. We may
then aggregate the data into congressional districts, which
permits comparisons of economic status with votes in the
House of Representatives. Thus, our pulse-taking can be

quite accurate at the congressional level.

Hence, the county figures of net gain or net loss
under both scenarios were amalagamated into congressional
districts for 1850 and 1860 and then converted into percentages. First, using the Congressional Directory, which
lists every county in each congressional district, we took
the 1850 Directory and aggregated the approximately 715
counties into 69 congressional districts; similarly, for
1860, 970 counties reduced to 66 congressional districts.[14]
Due to lags in redistricting the congressional district
configuration based on the 1850 Census was, in effect, for
the period 1842-1852; the 1860 pattern reflects the period
from 1853 to 1862.[15] Then, for each congressional district,
the sums of the gains and losses from every county comprising
the district was divided by the total wealth of the district,
yielding the percentage change in total wealth for each
congressional district in 1850 and 1860.

Maps III and IV, which illustrate the patterns of
losses and gains in congressional districts under scenario
1 (under scenario 2, all were gainers) can be compared with
the county Maps I and II to ascertain that aggregation at

---

[14] Congressional Directory, Washington D.C. 1850;
Congressional Directory, Washington D.C. 1860.

[15] Emanuel Celler, "Congressional Apportionment --
Past, Present and Future." Law and Contemporary Problems, 17
(1952) 270-271; Robert B. McKay, Reapportionment: the Law
and Politics of Equal Representation, (Twentieth Century Fund;
New York, 1965)

MAP III

Pattern of Impact from a 10% Land Reduction
on Southern Congressional Districts, 1850,
Under Scenario 1.

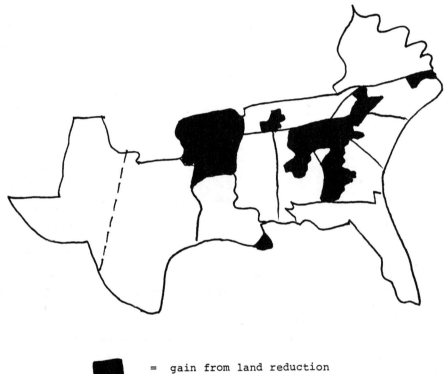

■ = gain from land reduction

□ = loss from land reduction

MAP IV

Pattern of Impact from a 10% Land Reduction
on Southern Congressional Districts, 1860,
Under Scenario 1.

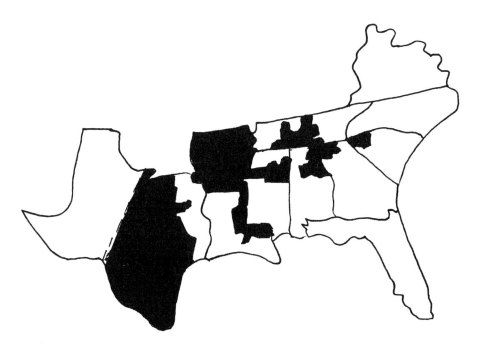

■ = gain from land reduction

☐ = loss from land reduction

congressional district level does not distort the county
pattern. Here again, Maps III and IV give a picture of slave
rich congressional districts as opposed to land rich congressional districts and the same westward drift of land
wealth between 1850 and 1860.

Although our economic data encompass the period
1840 to 1860, the political data limit our observations.
During this period there were ten roll calls on land distribution bills in the House of Representatives. Unfortunately, six of them occured in 1859-1860, and involved solid
bloc voting from the South. Obviously these roll calls
were too close to the actual declaration of the Civil War
to be useful. The same is true of the two roll calls in
1854 -- voting here was heavily tainted by the passions of
the Kansas-Nebraska Act which was debated during the same
session of Congress. We were left, however, with two
solid roll calls. The first, a roll call on a graduation
bill in 1846, presents a classic land distribution problem;
and the second, an early roll call on a homestead bill
involves both a more dramatic and difficult distribution
problem.

The graduation bill of 1846 was reported out of
committee in the House on January 21st. It provided that
the price of land unsold for ten or more years be reduced
to $1.00 an acre;   land unsold for 15 or more years be
reduced to $.75 an acre;   and land on the market for 20

or more years be reduced to $.50 per acre.[16] The House did
not begin consideration of the bill until July 6th and
passed it on July 14th, in a more conservative form, by a
vote of 92 to 89.[17] After restricting the total amount of
land which could be bought for $.50, the Senate passed the
bill.[18] However, the bill with its Senate amendment was
not acted on by the House during the second session and
appears to have been dropped from active consideration until
the 33rd Congress.

The economic interests on the graduation bill are
so straightforward as to be almost a textbook case. Here
was a scheme to distribute the public lands rapidly by
reducing the prices on a portion of them. The economic
interest of land rich Congressional districts should have
been clear -- this bill, if passed, would have hurt them.
Symmetrically, the interests of slave rich districts would
dictate a favorable position on a bill which increased
the supply of land, hence the marginal physical product of
slaves, and hence their value. Thus, under scenario 1 one
would expect slave rich districts to vote in favor of and

[16] Cong. Globe, 29 Cong., 1 sess., 209.

[17] Cong. Globe, 29 Cong., 1059=1094. The $1.00
minimum price was restricted to land on the market 20
or more years; $.75 for 25 or more years; $.50 for 30
or more years.

[18] Cong. Globe, 29 Cong., 1 sess., 1180.

and land rich districts to vote against this bill. Under
scenario 2, the reality scenario in which all districts
are relative losers from land expansion, we would expect
that the relatively greater losers would vote against this
bill.

Economic interests on the homestead bill of 1852 were
not quite as simple. The bill was introduced in the House
on December 10, 1851. The House considered it throughout
March and May of 1852 until it passed on May 12th by a vote
of 107 to 56.[19] The Senate, however, refused on three
occasions -- August 12th, 20th, and February 21st -- to
take up consideration.[20]

For this bill, the economic interests are perverse.
It was generally believed that homestead, as a grant of
free land, would not only result in rapid distribution of
land, but also in settlement by those who could neither
afford slaves nor approved of slavery. Thus, a slave rich
congressional district might very well have perceived that
its economic interests would not be served by homestead.
Why favor a bill which would populate territory with people
outside one's own financial market and political persuasion?
Hence, we would expect slave rich districts to have voted

---

[19] Cong. Globe, 32 Cong., 1 sess., 58, 670, 685,
707, 723, 926, 1275-1284, 1311-1320, 1351.

[20] Cong. Globe, 32 Cong., 1 sess., 2194-2267;
2 sess., 747.

against the homestead bill under scenario 1.[21] And

under scenario 2, again, one would expect that the

relatively greater losers would vote against homestead

-- the slave rich losers this time, not the land rich

loser as with the graduation bill.

Thus, we have both a set of data and a set of

hypotheses about the influence of the distribution of

wealth on two congressional roll call votes. There are

a number of possible statistical tests of these hypotheses.

Largely on grounds of efficiency and intuitive appeal,

---

[21] Note that we have no strong hypothesis
about the economic interests of land rich congressional
districts and the homestead bill. A hypothesis, however is not necessary in order to expect a significant
relationship between voting and relative wealth holding.
Further, we understand that the enemies of homestead
are actually no different from those of graduation,
but we emphasize, again, that it is perception, not
reality, we are looking at. And the perception of
slaveowners that homestead would hurt the market for
slaves is not an unreasonable one.

economists often prefer the technique of linear regression.[22]

---

[22] For those unfamiliar with linear regression, there is an intuitive explanation: linear regression is a method of finding a constant term and one or more coefficients in the right-hand side of a linear equation which best predict variations in the left-hand side (dependent) variable. The coefficients and constant terms, called parameters, are chosen by finding the numbers which minimize the sum of the squared "residual" (or unexplained) variations. In two dimensions, this would mean fitting a line through a set of observations which minimizes the sum of the squared distances, r_1, r_2, r_3, etc., in Figure A:

FIGURE A

Y
Fatalities per
Passenger Mile

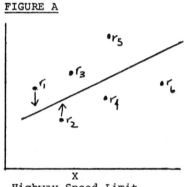

X
Highway Speed Limit

This curve fitting surely has an intuitive meaning. The variable X is causing the variable Y to change value. The fitted relationship is not exact, however, because of errors in observation in data and other road maintenance, traffic density, etc.

Less intuitive, but as important, is what the linear regression equation indicates about the probability that the relationship it describes is a true one. Goodness of fit of the parameters estimated by linear regression (the coefficients, or slope of the line, and the constant, the point at which it intersects the Y axis) give statisticians ways of

(continued)

For both votes, we have estimated the coefficients of the
following four relationships:

$$\text{(i)} \quad V = a_1 + b_1 \, SC_1 + z_1 \qquad\qquad (29)$$

$$\text{(ii)} \quad V = a_2 + b_2 \, SC_1 + b_3 W + z_2$$

$$\text{(iii)} \quad V = a_3 + b_4 \, SC_2 + z_3$$

$$\text{(iv)} \quad V = a_4 + b_5 \, SC_2 + b_6 W + z_4$$

where:

$V = 1$ for a "yes" vote.

$V = 2$ for a "no" vote.

SC_1 = the percentage gain or loss in wealth associated with a 10% decrease in land under
scenario 1.

SC_2 = the percentage gain associated with a 10%
decrease in land under scenario 2.

$W = 1$ for western districts: all congressional
districts in Alabama, Arkansas, Florida,
Louisiana, Mississippi, Tennessee and
Texas.

$W = 2$ for nonwestern districts: all congressional
districts in Georgia, North Carolina, South
Carolina and Virginia.

z = a random error term with the mean = 0.

The dummy variable (W) for westerness is included in the
relationships (ii) and (iv) to test the hypothesis that

(footnote 22 continued from previous page)
interpreting the probability that the real parameter actually
falls within the hypothesized range.

In conclusion, then, linear regression permits us to (1)
fit a line which describes the relationship between variables,
and (2) to estimate the probability that random errors, not
the relationship itself, caused the observed fit.

the South was split on traditional East-West lines on land
votes. However, the possible influence of westerness on
voting behavior does not preclude testing the hypothesized
influence of the distribution of southern slave and land
wealth; the equations are multivariate in that they admit
the possibility that both influences were at work.

The least squares regression estimates for the
1846 roll call vote, based on 58 observations, is presented
at Table VII. The t-statistics are shown in parentheses.

Three conclusions may be drawn for Table VII. First,
the hypothesis that southern political behavior corresponded
with the pattern of wealth-holding is confirmed; moreover,
that the distribution of wealth had the political impact
expected under the assumptions of the perception scenario,
SC_1. The sign of the coefficient is positive indicating
that land rich districts voted against the bill, slave rich
districts voted in favor, and the t-statistics of the coefficient estimates for SC_1 in (i) and (ii) are just short of
significance at th 90% confidence level. Second, the
regressions show that there was no relationship between voting
behavior and the impact of the bill on wealth patterns under
the assumptions of the reality scenario, SC_2. This would
suggest that southerners did not understand the real economic
paradoxes associated with land expansion. Third, the regressions do not confirm any simple geographic split within

TABLE VII

Regression Estimates for the 1846
Graduation Bill Vote

(i) $V = 1.24 + \underset{(1.28)}{.064} SC_1$

(ii) $V = 1.18 + \underset{(1.20)}{.061} SC_1 + \underset{(.74)}{.013} W$

(iii) $V = 1.19 + \underset{(.06)}{.0017} SC_2$

(iv) $V = 1.12 + \underset{(.028)}{.00077} SC_2 + \underset{(.84)}{.015} W$

the South on the graduation bill. As with SC_2, the t-
statistics for (ii) and (iv) show no significance.

The least squares estimate for the 1852 roll call
vote, based on 52 observations, is presented in Table VIII.
The t-statistics are shown in parentheses.

Here the relationship between the perceived impact
of the bill on slave rich districts and voting behavior is
shown quite clearly. As expected, the signs of the coefficients in SC_1 and SC_2 are negative: congressional districts
holding relatively more slave wealth than land wealth voted
against the homestead bill. Moreover, the t-statistics
for scenario 1 confirm the results in the graduation vote:
the t-stastics of the coefficients of SC_1 in (i) and (ii)
show them to be less than zero at the significance level
of 98%. In other words, the hypothesis, under the assumptions of the perception scenario, is confirmed. By con-
trast,the t-statistics for the coefficients for the reality
scenario, SC_2 in (iii) and (iv) show them to be less than
zero at the statistical significance level of 85% -- again
a bit too low to confirm the hypothesis that southerners
understood that all districts would lose from land expansion.
Here, too, westerness seems to have no measurable relationship with voting behavior.

Those versed in basic statistical methods may note
that the use of a dummy variable on the left-hand side of
the regressions in (i) through (iv) violates one of the

TABLE VIíI

Regression Estimates for the 1852
Homestead Bill Vote

(i) $V = 1.46 - .13\ SC_1$
         (-2.06)

(ii) $V = 1.41 - .13\ SC_1 + .011\ W$
         $(-2.06)\qquad (.46)$

(iii) $V = 1.66 - .035\ SC_2$
         (-1.07)

(iv) $V = 1.62 - .0355\ SC_2 = .010\ W$
         $(-1.07)\qquad\ (.39)$

conditions of the general linear model. By restricting
the range of the dependent variable to between 1 (yes) and
2 (no), we can no longer assume that the error terms are
distributed normally. Thus, it is not possible to make
rigorous statistical inferences from the standard error
of the coefficients. Nonetheless, regression in this case
still has strong intuitive properties and is frequently
used for that reason.

Alternative estimation procedures, however, do
exist which permit rigorous inferences about hypotheses.
One of these methods, called logit analysis, is based on the
intuitive concept that the left-hand side variable repre-
sents a probability, which varies form 0 to 1.0. The
assumed functional relationship between this probability
and the independent variables takes the form:

$$P = \frac{e^{XB}}{1 + e}XB \tag{30}$$

where:

e = the natural constant 2.718.

X = the independent variable.

$XB = B_0 + B_1X_1 + B_2X_2 \ldots \ldots + B_nX_n$

B = the coefficients of the independent variables to be estimated.

In other words, logit analysis estimates a set of

coefficients ($\hat{B}$) from a set of independent variables (X)
and a dependent variable (P) that must vary between 0
and 1. The exact mathematical properties of $\hat{B}$ are described in detail elsewhere;[23] what concerns us is the
fact that for estimates based on large samples one may
make statistical inferences about the way independent
variables influence dependent variables.

Table IX shows the estimated coefficients of the
independent variables for each of the eight combinations of
variables shown in Tables VII and VIII. The signs of these
coefficients should be interpreted exactly as the signs
of regression coefficients are interpreted. The t-statistics are shown in parentheses.

The broad outlines of the regression analysis
are confirmed by the logit analysis. In 1846, the positive
relationship between voting and SC_1 is significant at about
the 90% level. But no relationship can be discerned between SC_2 and voting behavior. Nor is any relationship
between westerness and voting behavior evident. In 1852,
as predicted, there is a strong negative relationship between
SC_1 and the dependent variable, voting behavior. Again, the
results for SC_2 are not particularly significant, and in
this case, are inconsistent. What is new, however, is the

---

[23] A.S. Goldberger, Econometric Theory (John
Wiley & Sons: New York, 1964) 248-251.

TABLE IX

Logit Analysis of the 1846 and 1852
Roll Call Votes

Vote	Constant	SC_1	SC_2	W
1846	-1.20	.41 (1.23)		
1846	-1.22	.41 (1.23)		.05 (.08)
1846	-1.51		.017 (.10)	
1846	-1.50		.016 (.09)	-.017 (.02)
1852	- .17	- .56 (-1.88)		
1852	-2.90	- .96 (-1.98)		5.04 (4.30)
1852	.74		-.15 (-1.10)	
1852	-3.30		.31 (1.07)	5.18 (3.99)

apparent significance of the coefficients of westerness,
at the 99% level, suggesting a very clear East-West conflict
on the Homestead issue. Southwestern congressional districts,
other things being equal, were more likely to vote in favor
of homestead than southeastern states. Nonetheless, this
in no way conflicts with the separate influence of wealth-
holding suggested by the significant coefficient of SC_1.

In conclusion, both regression and logit analysis
have confirmed two of the hypotheses: (1) the division of
wealth-holding in the South between relatively land rich and
relatively slave rich areas expressed itself in voting on
land distribution bills; (2) southern political behavior
was rational, from a profit maximizing point of view, vis-
a-vis political issues which would have affected the relative value of their wealth, under the assumption that the
demand curve for cotton was perfectly elastic.

Statistical testing did not confirm the other two
hypotheses: (1) voting behavior on the two land distribution
bills would suggest that the South did not act as if it
understood that, in economic reality, the demand curve for
cotton was not perfectly elastic; (2) out of eight equations
on the influence of westerness on voting behavior, only two
show t-statistics which are significant; this result is
probably too ambiguous to either confirm or reject the
hypothesis that geography influence voting behavior.

Thus, the results of the statistical analysis would point to the conclusion that relative slave versus land wealth was a more reasonable explanation for political conflict than was the geographic division between Southeast and Southwest. In fact, the significant results under the constraints of the perception scenario are strong enough to conclude that slave and land divisions were the central economic divisions.

CHAPTER IV

CONCLUSION

As demonstrated in Chapter I, a persistent historical debate over the profitability of slavery has yielded
to the methods of the new economic history. Much of the
power in these methods lay in the view that slaves could be
looked on as capital; hence, the system of plantation
slavery could be analyzed through the principles of capital
theory.

A subsidiary advance in the understanding of the
economics of slavery was made by Passell and Wright's
analysis of territorial expansion. Both the traditional
and new history's view of land expansion regarded land as
a factor which complimented slave labor and thus was an
economic necessity. Passell and Wright, going beyond this
partial analysis of the impact of land on slavery, also
considered the partial effect of land on the supply of
cotton. They then examined the impact land expansion would
have on the earnings of slaves and found that when cotton
land increased, the net impact on slave values was negative.
Defining the value of a slave as equal to the marginal
physical product times the price of cotton, discounted over
time by the opportunity cost of capital, Passell and Wright
found that increasing cotton land, thus increasing cotton

supply, lowered the price of cotton more than it raised
the MPP of slaves.

In addition, we argued that if land expansion
had a net negative impact on the value of slaves, then its
impact on the other major asset held by southerners, land,
would be a fortiori negative. The value of land is equal
to its MPP times the price of cotton, divided by the
discount rate. An increase in the supply of land would
drive down not only the price of cotton, but the MPP of
existing land as well.

This approach suggests an untraditional interpretation of the economics of land expansion. Far from being
an economic necessity, expansion appears to have had a
negative impact on southern wealth. Although this approach
is useful in evaluating the effect of land expansion in the
aggregate, it provides only a basic framework for the economic or political historian. Equally interesting questions
remain: who lost the most from expansion? Who gained the
most? Where were these groups located? How, if at all,
politically self-conscious were these groups? Did they
act politically in their own interest?

However, there is a major analytic problem in
answering those questions. Perceived economic interests of
southern wealthholders were not necessarily identical to
their actual economic interest. In this case, there is a
rather strong argument to be made that wealthholders would

not have understood the impact of the inelastic demand
for cotton.From the point of view of any cotton farmer operating
in a competitive market, the demand for cotton is, of course,
perfectly elastic. It is not unreasonable that such farmers
neglected the downward slope of the demand curve for the
industry in calculating the benefits or losses associated
with expansion. Hence, we hypothesized a perception
scenario, scenario 1, which assumed that land expansion
affected the value of land and slaves only in terms of
their respective MPP's, the price of cotton remaining unaffected. We also hypothesized a reality scenario, scenario
2, based on the assumption that land expansion affected the
value of land and slaves both in terms of their MPP's and
the price of cotton.

These two scenarios became the basis for an
empirical examination of the impact of land expansion on
southern wealth. Since land expansion has been presumed
necessary, and since the public lands were, in fact, distributed quite rapidly, we asked the counterfactual question:
what would have happened if 10% less land had been put into
cotton production in 1850 and 1860? For, to know what would
have happened in the absence of land expansion indicates
how important, and in what way, actual expansion was.

Given two scenarios, there are two related analyses.
First, the perception scenario asks which wealthholders
would have gained and which would have lost if 10% less

land had been sold in the South in 1850 and 1860 assuming
that the demand for cotton was perfectly elastic? Summar-
izing the theory explained in Chapter II, we note:

the value formulas for slaves:

$$V_S = \frac{MPP_S \cdot P_C - M}{i} \qquad (31)$$

and for land:

$$V_L = \frac{MPP_L \cdot P_C}{i} \qquad (32)$$

When rewritten in rates-of-change form, they become:

$$V_S{}^* = K(MPP_S{}^* + P_C{}^*) \qquad (33)$$

$$V_L{}^* = MMP_L{}^* + P_C{}^* \qquad (34)$$

Substituting in the estimates of $MPP_S{}^*$, $MPP_L{}^*$, $P_C{}^*$ and K
derived in Chapter II:

$$V_S{}^* = 1.1 \ (-3.2 + 0) = -3.52\% \qquad (35)$$

$$V_L{}^* = 6.8 + 0 = 6.8\% \qquad (36)$$

For the second part of the analysis, the reality scenario
asks who would have been the relative gainers if 10% less

land had been sold in the South in 1850 and 1860 assuming
that the demand for cotton was not perfectly elastic, so
we substituted a different value for P_C*:

$$V_S* = 1.1(-3.2 +4.9) = 1.87\% \tag{37}$$

$$V_L* = 6.8 + 4.9 = 11.7\% \tag{38}$$

The two positive estimates for V_S* and V_L* in scenario 2
indicated that everyone would have gained from a land
reduction because the decrease in the supply of cotton
would have pushed up the price of cotton sufficiently to
offset any decrease in the MPP of slaves. The question is
still, however, a significant one, because it is important
to understand who would have been the larger and smaller
gainers under this scenario; in other words, who had the
most, and the least, to lose from land expansion.

After calculating the percentage changes that a
10% decrease in land would have had on assets, we calculated how much of each asset was actually held by the South
in each county in 1850 and 1860. To make this calculation
for slave wealth, price scales based on age, sex and old-new
South were used along with the Population Schedule of the
U.S. Census for 1850 and 1860 to estimate total male and
female wealth for a random sample of counties in every

state. The figures from the sample counties were then used
to estimate an average male and female price for every
state, and the total number of males and of females in
every county of each state was multiplied by that state's
estimated average price. The male and female figures were
added together to obtain a single measure of slave wealth
in each county. The product of these calculations, then,
was estimates of total slave wealth weighted by age, sex
and location for every county in the South for 1850 and 1860.
An estimate of land wealth in each county was obtained
directly from the Agriculture Schedule of the U.S. Census
for 1850 and 1860.

These figures for actual wealth holdings were
multiplied by the measures of percentage changes under
scenario 1 and 2 for 1850 and 1860. The result of this
operation was a novel picture of changes in wealth holdings
related to varying ratios of slave and land wealth. Under
scenario 1, the perception scenario, an evenly scattered
pattern of gains and losses appeared. In 1850, southerners
who held relatively more of their wealth in land than in
slaves were almost uniformly distributed throughout the
South; in 1860, although the fulcrum of land rich areas
shifted westward, there were still areas in the Southeast
where wealth was held primarily in land rather than in slaves.
It was, of course, these relatively land rich southerners

who would have gained most from a 10% land reduction.
For, a land reduction meant an increase in the MPP of their
land and hence an increase in its value under scenario 1.
Under scenario 2, the gains would have been even greater
because a reduction in land would also have meant a decrease
in the supply of cotton and hence an increase in the price
of cotton, further increasing the value of existing land.

This picture of the South is a more sophisticated
and refined picture than the traditional one which depicts
an economic split on a straight sectional basis -- the land-
poor old South, or Southeast, versus the land-rich new South,
or Southwest. Instead, it appears that relatively land
rich areas were dotted throughout the South, old and new,
both in 1850 and 1860.

After these groups of economic assets were defined
and located geographically, we turned to the political
questions. Did these economic groups explain political
divisions? Did political behavior indicate that gainers
or losers understood their economic interests under either
scenario? It was expected that political awareness would
manifest itself under the assumptions of the perception
scenario. Nonetheless, looking for political awareness on
the basis of the reality scenario is important. Southern
wealthholders may have understood that they all stood to
lose from land expansion. The fact that some had much more

to lose than others might still have led to a divergence
of political behavior.

The traditional view of intrasectional southern
politics is as rough as the traditional view of intrasectional economics. Most historians characterize voting
in the South between 1840 and 1860 as split along strict
sectional lines; the Southeast voting against measures
to distribute the public lands and the Southwest voting
in favor. However, since the economic picture of the South
as a geographically split entity proved to be misleading,
the political picture, as well, might prove to be wrong.
We tested hypotheses that political divisions were based
on economic interests.

To hold the political data as close to the
disaggregated realities of the economic data, votes in the
Senate were rejected as too general. As an alternative,
county economic figures were aggregated into congressional
districts for 1850 and 1860 in order to look at voting in
the House of Representatives.

Although there were ten congressional roll calls
on land distribution bills during the period 1843-1860, only
two of them were sufficiently "neutral" to use: six of then
transpired on the eve of the Civil War and the other two
occurred in the middle of the Kansas-Nebraska debates. The
first useable roll call was a vote on a graduation bill in

1846, and the second was a vote on a homestead bill in 1852. The graduation bill presented a straightforward distribution problem. The bill provided for sale, at reduced prices, land which had been on the market for a number of years; hence, land rich congressional districts should have been against this bill and slave rich districts would have been more likely to favor it. The homestead bill, however, was not so straightforward. With homestead, a scheme to distribute land free to settlers, it is reasonable to expect slave rich districts to oppose passage on the grounds that homestead would ultimately harm the cause of slavery; homesteaders would neither buy slaves nor feel politically beholden to the slave system.

A first test used for political and economic correspondence was based on linear regression analysis. This test asked if the independent variables of economic gain or loss, and of westerness or nonwesterness, were able to explain variations in the dependent variable, congressional voting behavior on the two bills. Coefficients of four relationships, for both bills, were estimated:

$$\text{(i)} \quad V = a_1 + b_1\, SC_1 + z_1 \tag{39}$$

$$\text{(ii)} \quad V = a_2 + b_2\, SC_1 + b_3 W + z_2$$

$$\text{(iii)} \quad V = a_3 + b_4\, SC_2 + z_3$$

(iv) $V = a_4 + b_5 \, SC_2 + b_6 W + z_4$

where:

V = 1 for a "yes" vote.

V = 2 for a "no" vote.

SC_1 = the percentage gain or loss in wealth associated with a 10% decrease in land under scenario 1.

SC_2 = the percentage gain in wealth associated with a 10% decrease in land under scenario 2.

W = 1 for western districts: all congressional districts in Alabama, Arkansas, Florida, Louisiana, Mississippi, Tennessee and Texas.

W = 2 for nonwestern districts: all congressional districts in Georgia, North Carolina, South Carolina and Virginia.

z = a random error term with the mean = 0.

For the graduation bill, the results of the linear regression confirmed the hypothesis that land rich and slave rich districts voted in harmony with their economic interests under scenario 1. The other hypotheses -- that voting corresponded either to economic interests under scenario 2, or to westerness -- were rejected. For the homestead bill, the results confirmed the hypothesis that slave rich congressional districts would vote against the bill under scenario 1. And, as in the case of the graduation bill, the results did not confirm any significant relationship between voting and scenario 2 or westerness.

A second estimation procedure, logit analysis, was

also used to test the hypotheses. Logit analysis permits
more rigorous inferences from the values of the test
statistics. The results of the logit analysis confirmed
the results obtained from the linear regression analysis.
For both roll call votes in 1846 and 1852, southern congressional districts voted in accord with their economic interests
under scenario 1. There was no confirmation of the hypothesis
that voting corresponded to economic interest under scenario
2, and only on the homestead roll call did the westerness
variable show any significance.

Hence, the empirical and statistical analysis points
to two conclusions about the economics of the antebellum
South. First, the view which holds that the South was
economically and politically split along east-west, new-old
lines is not consistent with the data. Instead, the economic
division of the South seems to have been between land rich
areas and slave rich areas, an economic division which
translated into observable political behavior. Moreover,
this division of the South violates the traditional geographic categories since slave rich and land rich areas can be
found throughout the South. Second, voting behavior shows
that southern congressional districts voted in accord with
their economic interests under scenario 1, the perception
scenario; thus, the argument that southerners were not
"economic men" appears to have been weakened.

This dissertation did not deal with the greater

political issue of territorial expansion. One certainly
might argue that the slave system had to expand its territory,
thereby its political influence, in order to ultimately
uphold its greater economic interest, the very system of
slave labor. Rather, we have looked at the intrasectional
issue of territorial expansion -- the impact of expansion
on southern wealth -- and we have found that expansion was
damaging to wealthholders who were relatively richer in
land than in slaves; that these land rich areas could be
found in both the Southeast and Southwest; and that on
political issues which directly affected this type of
wealth holding, southerners acted in an economically rational
fashion.

APPENDIX

<u>Wealth Holdings in Southern States, in Dollars</u>

<u>for 1850 and 1860</u>

Wealth Holdings in 1850, in Dollars

State: Alabama

County	Male Slaves	Female Slaves	Slave Totals	Land
Autauga	2,555,371	2,446,056	5,001,428	1,418,693
Baldwin	852,065	1,946,964	2,799,029	126,757
Barbour	3,524,645	3,040,417	6,565,062	2,025,933
Benton	1,269,712	1,060,407	2,330,119	1,360,224
Bibb	963,078	775,537	1,738,615	651,591
Blount	125,856	110,950	236,806	261,857
Butler	1,164,239	967,527	2,131,766	428,653
Calhoun*				
Chambers	3,791,074	3,143,005	6,934,079	2,346,643
Cherokee	557,026	486,233	1,043,259	1,212,968
Choctaw	1,316,791	1,024,818	2,341,609	675,021

*	= did not exist in 1850
**	= did not exist in 1860
***	= no record

Wealth Holdings in 1850 (continued)

State: Alabama

County	Male Slaves	Female Slaves	Slave Totals	Land
Clarke	1,689,972	1,339,946	3,029,918	715,506
Coffee	169,652	164,958	334,610	251,561
Conecuh	1,411,438	980,261	2,391,699	463,436
Coosa	1,292,379	1,052,835	2,345,214	864,681
Covington	154,466	137,981	292,447	105,213
Dale	240,661	216,598	457,259	325,499
Dallas	7,823,333	6,209,819	14,033,152	4,101,623
Dekalb	162,974	152,762	315,736	476,075
Fayette	346,519	354,489	701,008	451,540
Franklin	2,826,131	2,294,887	5,121,018	2,260,432
Greene	7,617,841	6,025,233	13,643,074	3,816,671
Hancock	26,075	19,013	45,088	43,089
Henry	800,984	591,804	1,392,788	650,677
Jackson	752,857	645,987	1,398,844	980,430

Wealth Holdings in 1850 (continued)

State: Alabama

County	Male Slaves	Female Slaves	Slave Totals	Land
Jefferson	707,525	645,644	1,353,169	636,329
Lauderdale	2,071,331	1,640,392	3,711,723	1,672,150
Lawrence	2,215,921	1,984,124	4,200,046	1,658,992
Limestone	2,666,545	2,225,973	4,892,518	2,040,170
Lowndes	5,038,630	4,079,782	9,118,412	1,883,192
Macon	5,310,032	4,512,373	9,822,405	2,553,259
Madison	4,750,387	3,964,930	5,152,967	3,292,600
Marengo	7,443,544	5,632,404	13,075,947	3,631,644
Marion	283,647	265,011	548,658	291,966
Marshall	278,017	254,401	532,418	436,731
Mobile	3,423,844	2,015,312	5,439,156	498,422
Monroe	2,269,245	1,766,402	4,035,647	883,387
Montgomery	6,889,277	4,613,585	11,502,862	2,953,744
Morgan	1,117,411	947,131	2,064,542	919,460

Wealth Holdings in 1850 (continued)

State: Alabama

County	Male Slaves	Female Slaves	Slave Totals	Land
Perry	5,039,391	3,887,676	8,927,067	2,705,451
Pickens	3,688,164	2,939,854	6,628,018	1,858,560
Pike	1,250,727	1,061,049	2,311,776	1,036,179
Randolph	292,769	267,560	560,329	633,456
Russell	3,865,512	3,118,600	6,984,112	1,801,413
St. Clair	521,451	308,304	829,755	405,198
Shelby	763,593	645,854	1,409,447	685,031
Sumter	5,157,158	4,062,804	9,219,962	1,840,874
Talladega	2,241,193	1,906,409	4,147,602	1,652,125
Tallapoosa	1,360,950	1,181,806	2,542,756	1,059,833
Tuscaloosa	2,570,424	2,063,124	4,633,548	1,174,818
Walker	87,815	72,672	160,487	259,260
Washington	515,437	412,297	927,734	183,914
Wilcox	4,010,172	3,219,037	7,229,209	2,033,447

Wealth Holdings in 1850   (continued)

State: Alabama

County	Male Slaves	Female Slaves	Slave Totals	Land
Winston*				

State: Arkansas

County	Male Slaves	Female Slaves	Slave Totals	Land
Arkansas	612,452	416,844	1,029,296	556,912
Ashley	226,565	177,209	403,774	165,582
Benton	62,173	52,967	115,140	222,520
Bradley	395,498	344,647	740,145	311,586
Calhoun*				
Carroll	60,525	63,026	123,551	190,721
Chicot	1,315,282	1,203,648	2,518,930	1,347,153
Clark	333,080	265,737	598,817	300,293
Columbia*				
Conway	82,940	70,248	153,188	159,801
Craighead*				

Wealth Holdings in 1850   (continued)

State: Arkansas

County	Male Slaves	Female Slaves	Slave Totals	Land
Crawford	302,395	325,263	627,658	408,198
Crittenden	327,974	211,080	539,054	485,808
Dallas	948,535	686,542	1,635,077	551,010
Desha	419,442	309,889	729,331	398,451
Drew	309,848	257,153	567,001	163,600
Franklin	162,143	133,490	295,633	223,561
Fulton	14,885	14,724	29,609	78,715
Greene	14,075	18,196	32,271	80,738
Hempstead	847,322	708,055	1,555,377	646,556
Hot Springs	119,485	106,563	226,048	203,956
Independence	275,824	233,299	275,823	535,669

* = did not exist in 1850
** = did not exist in 1860
***= no record

Wealth Holdings in 1850   (continued)

State: Arkansas

County	Male Slaves	Female Slaves	Slave Totals	Land
Izard	67,831	53,428	121,259	151,892
Jackson	197,815	167,444	510,269	254,219
Jefferson	960,542	746,389	1,706,931	846,969
Johnson	239,627	210,702	450,339	332,953
LaFayette	1,278,234	894,185	2,172,419	491,937
Lawrence	121,846	118,885	240,731	284,378
Madison	54,406	47,365	101,771	274,289
Marion	42,580	30,000	72,580	145,450
Mississippi	297,777	244,957	542,734	330,774
Monroe	136,340	118,815	255,155	99,794
Montgomery	22,485	24,964	47,449	108,082
Newton	12,957	14,375	27,332	68,011
Owachita	1,165,154	924,604	2,089,758	336,724
Perry	4,847	4,610	9,458	27,025

Wealth Holdings in 1850 (continued)

State: Arkansas

County	Male Slaves	Female Slaves	Slave Totals	Land
Phillips	957,336	7,782,841	1,735,619	1,043,304
Pike	38,033	33,325	71,358	88,131
Poinsett	104,726	72,378	177,104	111,592
Polk	23,819	19,670	43,489	55,538
Pope	157,784	133,295	291,079	279,684
Praire	94,863	82,870	177,733	189,115
Pulaski	375,241	347,629	722,870	439,068
Randolph	77,568	73,615	151,183	181,792
St. Francis	265,954	216,612	482,566	289,589
Saline	170,427	137,067	307,494	242,953
Scott	46,464	45,842	128,953	110,446
Searcy	6,035	10,100	16,135	92,425
Sebastian*				
Sevier	470,733	399,577	870,310	253,002

Wealth Holdings in 1850 (continued)

State: Arkansas

County	Male Slaves	Female Slaves	Slave Totals	Land
Union	1,689,713	1,375,640	3,065,353	728,517
Van Buren	25,733	35,051	60,784	139,818
Washington	370,400	390,287	760,688	775,558
White	94,598	96,372	190,970	165,140
Yell	110,349	121,469	231,818	222,915

State: Florida

County	Male Slaves	Female Slaves	Slave Totals	Land
Alachua	298,504	245,055	543,559	179,941
Benton	113,637	84,549	198,187	81,547
Brevard*				
Calhoun	160,755	119,686	280,442	154,281
Clay*				
Columbia	444,849	336,001	780,850	260,856
Dade	2,772	3,843	6,615	2,185

Wealth Holdings in 1850   (continued)

State: Florida

County	Male Slaves	Female Slaves	Slave Totals	Land
Duval	722,387	531,097	1,253,485	300,683
Escambia	1,793,256	366,746	2,160,002	33,711
Franklin	139,275	94,432	233,707	***
Gadsden	1,629,729	1,366,513	2,996,242	954,699
Hamilton	221,732	196,000	417,732	129,439
Hillsborough	253,604	171,328	424,932	235,274
Holmes	53,354	46,667	100,021	21,735
Jackson	1,222,297	944,865	2,167,162	420,311
Jefferson	1,678,926	1,353,886	3,032,812	567,212
Lafayette*				
Leon	2,810,451	2,218,594	5,029,045	1,748,510
Levy	43,461	42,595	86,055	32,314

*   = did not exist in 1850
**   = did not exist in 1860
*** = no record

Wealth Holdings in 1850   (continued)

State: Florida

County	Male Slaves	Female Slaves	Slave Totals	Land
Liberty*				
Madison	995,022	696,708	1,691,730	521,165
Manatex*				
Marion	437,227	182,275	619,502	359,651
Monroe	160,063	107,608	267,671	4,230
Nassau	358,928	303,059	924,797	103,271
New River*				
Orange	79,573	60,881	140,454	70,390
Putnam	79,685	48,863	128,548	33,483
Santa Rosa	311,117	181,177	492,294	60,243
St. Lucie	11,086	6,040	17,126	***
St. Johns	305,574	286,587	592,162	165,580
Suwawnee*				
Sumter*				

Wealth Holdings in 1850 (continued)

State: Florida

County	Male Slaves	Female Slaves	Slave Totals	Land
Taylor *				
Volusia *				
Wakulla	271,989	214,740	486,729	67,260
Walton	270,236	213,020	483,256	45,203
Washington	168,378	142,746	311,123	79,634

State: Georgia

County	Male Slaves	Female Slaves	Slave Totals	Land
Appling	93,575	78,812	172,387	146,434
Baker	912,285	763,416	1,675,701	1,542,925
Baldwin	1,087,370	952,200	2,039,570	667,735
Banks *				
Berrien *				
Bibb	1,262,455	1,222,542	2,484,997	920,133
Brooks *				

143

Wealth Holdings in 1850   (continued)

State: Georgia

County	Male Slaves	Female Slaves	Slave Totals	Land
Bryan	520,405	469,062	989,467	313,453
Bullock	349,200	301,392	650,592	350,366
Burke	2,629,670	2,167,290	4,796,960	2,320,317
Butts	671,240	579,600	1,250,840	681,734
Calhoun *				
Camden	951,570	914,526	1,866,096	894,776
Campbell	349,685	320,436	670,121	871,072
Carroll	255,650	222,216	477,866	
Cass	734,290	609,822	1,344,112	1,506,668
Catoosa *				
Charlton *				
Chatham	3,164,625	2,997,360	6,161,985	2,128,791
Chattahuechee *				
Chattooga	401,580	349,002	750,582	793,265

Wealth Holdings in 1850   (continued)

State: Georgia

County	Male Slaves	Female Slaves	Slave Totals	Land
Cherokee	262,385	252,954	515,339	930,462
Clark	1,320,655	1,157,958	2,478,613	1,079,486
Clay*				
Clayton*				
Clinch	29,585	27,324	56,909	58,241
Cobb	520,890	487,692	1,008,582	768,163
Coffee*				
Colquit*				
Columbia	1,981,225	1,689,534	3,670,759	1,541,983
Cowetta	1,281,370	1,134,774	2,416,144	1,873,294
Crawford	1,174,455	913,284	2,087,739	1,134,714

*   = did not exist in 1850
**   = did not exist in 1860
*** = no record

Wealth Holdings in 1850   (continued)

State: Georgia

County	Male Slaves	Female Slaves	Slave Totals	Land
Dade	32,495	33,534	66,029	236,796
Dawson *				
Decatur	879,790	746,442	1,626,232	749,879
Dekalb	663,480	631,350	1,294,830	1,137,168
Dooly	636,320	599,886	1,236,206	478,383
Dougherty *				
Early	818,195	740,232	1,558,518	728,728
Eckols *				
Effingham	475,300	347,760	823,060	314,084
Elbert	1,519,990	1,272,636	2,792,626	1,590,491
Emanuel	238,620	395,784	634,404	576,292
Fannin *				
Fayette	469,480	406,134	875,614	996,015
Floyd	708,045	605,784	1,313,829	1,080,923

Wealth Holdings in 1850 (continued)

State: Georgia

County	Male Slaves	Female Slaves	Slave Totals	Land
Forsythe	699,855	639,216	1,339,071	728,421
Franklin	546,110	506,322	1,052,432	1,106,309
Fulton*				
Gilmer	45,590	43,884	89,474	488,031
Glasscock*				
Glynn	934,595	914,526	1,849,121	761,666
Gordon	194,970	173,466	368,436	587,141
Greene	2,006,445	1,672,974	3,679,419	1,771,624
Gwinnet	549,020	473,202	1,022,222	989,347
Habersham	289,060	251,298	540,358	476,841
Hall	321,555	272,412	593,967	605,194
Hancock	1,807,080	1,379,000	3,186,080	1,349,412
Haralson*				
Harris	1,802,260	1,461,834	3,264,094	1,663,270

Wealth Holdings in 1850   (continued)

State: Georgia

County	Male Slaves	Female Slaves	Slave Totals	Land
Hart*				
Heard	558,720	508,806	1,067,526	741,734
Henry	1,141,205	1,065,636	2,206,841	1,761,998
Houston	2,388,625	2,031,498	4,420,123	2,728,972
Irwin	106,215	95,220	201,435	102,957
Jackson	668,815	630,522	1,299,337	753,601
Jasper	1,726,600	1,448,586	3,175,186	1,472,337
Jefferson	1,285,250	1,081,782	2,367,032	1,392,598
Johnson*				
Jones	1,497,195	1,298,718	2,795,913	1,257,906
Laurens	701,555	559,780	1,261,335	422,332
Lee	868,635	741,888	1,610,523	1,059,726
Liberty	1,396,800	1,223,784	2,620,584	777,137
Lincoln	920,530	760,104	1,680,634	649,034

Wealth Holdings in 1850   (continued)

State: Georgia

County	Male Slaves	Female Slaves	Slave Totals	Land
Lowndes	555,810	497,214	1,053,024	857,110
Lumpkin	237,165	182,574	419,739	624,109
Macon	674,150	638,802	1,312,952	1,082,250
Madison	445,230	411,102	856,332	589,251
Marion	861,845	747,270	1,609,115	1,166,442
McIntosh	1,103,860	938,124	2,041,984	760,948
Meriweather	1,958,325	1,642,225	3,600,550	2,091,976
Miller *				
Milton *				
Mitchell *				
Monroe	2,448,765	2,113,056	4,561,821	2,473,856
Montgomery	137,255	158,976	296,231	121,754
Morgan	1,697,500	1,449,000	3,146,500	1,378,614
Murray	462,205	381,708	843,913	1,613,669

Wealth Holdings in 1850   (continued)

State: Georgia

County	Male Slaves	Female Slaves	Slave Totals	Land
Muscogee	1,892,955	1,728,864	3,621,819	1,645,749
Newton	1,259,545	1,055,286	2,314,831	1,236,736
Oglethorpe	1,796,440	1,692,846	3,489,286	1,887,370
Paulding	344,350	312,156	656,506	733,877
Pickens *				
Pierce *				
Pike	1,297,860	1,176,588	2,474,448	1,676,436
Polk *				
Pulaski	662,090	561,285	1,223,375	729,765
Putnam	1,836,210	1,492,884	3,329,094	1,134,950
Quitman *				

*   = did not exist in 1850
**   = did not exist in 1860
***   = no record

151

Wealth Holdings in 1850   (continued)

State: Georgia

County	Male Slaves	Female Slaves	Slave Totals	Land
Rabun	25,220	22,770	47,990	160,641
Randolph	1,172,245	1,058,184	2,230,429	1,360,494
Richmond	1,799,835	1,658,898	3,458,733	1,167,741
Schley*				
Scriven	908,890	727,398	1,636,288	626,416
Spalding*				
Stewart	1,754,245	1,533,456	3,287,701	2,259,837
Sumter	924,895	787,842	1,712,737	1,271,594
Talbot	2,080,650	1,808,352	3,889,002	2,128,177
Taliaferro	737,200	618,930	1,356,130	625,451
Tatnall	203,145	158,335	361,480	233,553
Taylor*				
Telfair	224,555	188,784	413,339	173,209
Terrell*				

Wealth Holdings in 1850 (continued)

State: Georgia

County	Male Slaves	Female Slaves	Slave Totals	Land
Thomas	1,183,885	1,110,348	2,294,233	1,163,790
Towns*				
Troud	2,111,690	1,911,438	4,023,128	2,028,248
Twiggs	1,143,145	909,972	2,053,117	784,799
Union	67,900	55,890	123,790	481,734
Upson	1,168,365	937,710	2,106,075	1,015,483
Walker	381,210	356,040	737,250	847,982
Walton	914,710	821,376	1,736,086	1,041,815
Ware	64,990	62,514	127,504	174,682
Warren	1,462,400	1,207,270	2,669,670	1,702,298
Washington	1,419,595	1,130,634	2,550,229	1,356,979
Wayne	88,755	89,424	178,179	92,272
Webster*				
White*				

Wealth Holdings in 1850   (continued)

State: Georgia

County	Male Slaves	Female Slaves	Slave Totals	Land
Whitfield*				
Wilcox*				
Wilkes	1,950,185	1,730,520	3,680,705	1,371,202
Wilkinson Worth*	634,380	579,186	1,213,566	942,198
State: Louisiana				
Ascension	2,577,062	1,945,786	4,522,848	6,551,959
Assumption	2,202,252	1,357,762	3,560,014	5,520,299
Avoyelles	1,934,772	3,019,072	4,953,844	1,296,500
Baton Rouge East	2,414,007	1,788,472	4,202,470	2,262,175
Baton Rouge West	1,699,984	1,160,280	2,860,264	2,107,835
Blenville	689,504	559,630	1,249,134	277,139

Wealth Holdings in 1850   (continued)

State: Louisiana

County	Male Slaves	Female Slaves	Slave Totals	Land
Bossier	1,679,180	1,269,862	2,949,042	743,804
Caddo	1,957,062	1,488,440	3,445,502	929,127
Calcasieu	339,551	253,152	592,703	144,737
Caldwell	424,056	363,844	787,900	232,379
Carroll	2,438,526	1,828,906	4,267,432	2,686,549
Catahoula	1,349,288	994,442	2,343,730	766,154
Clairborne	904,231	759,456	1,663,687	423,727
Concordia	2,615,360	1,951,380	4,566,740	2,567,564
De Soto	1,675,465	1,264,002	2,939,467	711,868
Feliciana East	3,406,655	2,833,896	6,240,551	1,589,574
Feliciana West	3,822,735	3,155,610	6,978,345	3,147,012
Franklin	553,535	483,450	1,036,985	345,913
Iberville	3,079,598	2,070,870	5,150,468	4,718,128
Jackson	770,491	655,148	1,425,639	309,452

Wealth Holdings in 1850   (continued)

State: Louisiana

County	Male Slaves	Female Slaves	Slave Totals	Land
Jefferson	2,486,821	1,616,188	4,103,009	1,676,174
Lafayette	1,216,291	887,204	2,103,495	380,356
Lafourche	1,777,999	1,138,598	2,916,597	2,281,024
Livingston	320,233	236,744	556,977	227,063
Madison	2,815,227	2,055,688	4,870,915	2,690,631
Morehouse	706,593	612,370	1,318,963	339,209
Natchitoches	2,920,733	2,273,680	5,194,413	1,554,464
Orleans	5,655,076	6,588,485	12,243,561	532,864
Ouichita	963,671	809,266	1,772,937	639,662
Plaquemines	1,873,103	1,277,480	3,150,583	5,215,618
Point Coupee	2,995,033	2,133,626	5,128,659	2,343,955

*   = did not exist in 1850
**   = did not exist in 1860
*** = no record

Wealth Holdings in 1850 (continued)

State: Louisiana

County	Male Slaves	Female Slaves	Slave Totals	Land
Rapides	4,338,277	3,174,362	7,512,739	2,946,056
Sabine	425,739	341,052	766,791	241,889
St. Bernard	1,150,907	437,156	1,588,063	1,114,159
St. Charles	1,765,368	1,012,022	2,777,390	2,173,040
St. Helena	787,580	656,906	1,444,486	285,907
St. James	3,397,616	1,895,983	5,293,599	2,848,463
St. John the Baptist	1,920,655	590,102	2,510,757	2,177,916
St. Landry	4,116,963	3,059,506	7,176,469	2,009,968
St. Martin's	2,490,536	1,783,784	4,274,320	1,504,317
St. Mary's	4,024,088	2,843,272	6,867,360	4,334,046
St. Tammany	975,559	602,994	1,578,553	145,258
Tensas	3,078,992	2,297,706	5,376,698	2,468,836
Terre Bonne	1,805,490	1,089,374	2,894,864	2,206,104

Wealth Holdings in 1850   (continued)

State: Louisiana

County	Male Slaves	Female Slaves	Slave Totals	Land
Union	1,184,342	1,065,348	2,249,690	480,527
Vermillion	379,044	285,600	664,644	133,380
Washington	372,243	310,580	682,823	117,737
Winn*				

State: Mississippi

County	Male Slaves	Female Slaves	Slave Totals	Land
Adams	4,817,603	3,878,463	8,696,066	2,330,123
Amite	2,247,744	1,660,078	3,907,822	480,434
Attala	1,233,536	968,426	2,201,962	849,605
Bolivar	837,568	581,282	1,418,850	776,185
Calhoun*				
Carroll	3,581,376	2,766,042	6,347,418	1,656,564
Chicksaw	2,395,680	1,802,710	4,198,390	1,403,566
Choctaw	1,044,384	873,338	1,917,722	561,367

158

Wealth Holdings in 1850 (continued)

State: Mississippi

County	Male Slaves	Female Slaves	Slave Totals	Land
Jackson	307,613	208,255	515,868	266,680
Jasper	646,944	565,434	1,212,378	286,640
Jefferson	3,838,076	2,944,332	6,783,308	1,753,966
Jones	94,208	80,372	174,580	60,252
Kemper	1,947,456	2,096,464	4,043,920	764,291
Lafayette	2,066,688	1,529,898	3,596,586	1,289,602
Lauderdale	993,808	800,324	1,704,132	409,621
Lawrence	1,050,272	828,624	1,878,896	421,613
Leake	546,848	451,102	997,950	229,650
Lowndes	4,767,072	3,629,192	8,396,264	2,255,002
Madison	5,015,840	3,921,248	8,937,088	1,975,865

*   = did not exist in 1850
**   = did not exist in 1860
***   = no record

Wealth Holdings in 1850   (continued)

State: Mississippi

County	Male Slaves	Female Slaves	Slave Totals	Land
Marion	744,746	544,764	1,289,510	231,493
Marshall	5,673,088	4,310,090	9,983,178	3,546,617
Monroe	4,305,600	3,851,630	8,157,230	2,503,381
Neshoba	458,528	396,200	854,728	266,309
Newton	351,808	311,300	663,108	225,173
Noxubee	4,275,424	3,081,304	7,356,728	1,743,586
Oktibbeha	1,739,168	1,387,266	3,126,434	731,546
Panola	2,332,384	1,816,860	4,149,244	1,260,216
Perry	279,680	202,628	482,308	91,426
Pike	1,124,608	874,470	1,999,078	430,765
Pontotoc	1,684,429	1,371,462	3,055,891	1,177,021
Rankin	1,158,464	953,144	2,111,608	594,550
Scott	406,272	353,184	750,456	158,734
Simpson	549,056	446,574	995,630	250,862

Wealth Holdings in 1850   (continued)

State: Mississippi

County	Male Slaves	Female Slaves	Slave Totals	Land
Smith	343,712	296,584	640,296	131,793
Sunflower	286,304	202,628	488,932	206,495
Tallahatchie	946,496	700,708	1,647,204	494,005
Tippah	1,757,568	1,420,094	3,177,662	1,461,826
Tishemongo	663,872	592,036	1,255,908	878,849
Tunica	373,888	228,098	601,986	271,456
Warren	4,814,104	3,481,206	8,295,310	2,152,365
Washington	2,967,552	2,120,802	5,088,354	3,449,957
Wayne	487,968	403,558	891,526	137,025
Wilkinson	4,714,816	3,792,200	8,507,016	1,826,872
Winston	988,448	790,702	1,779,150	483,671
Yalobusha	3,083,104	2,447,384	5,530,488	1,321,870
Yazoo	3,771,264	2,917,164	6,688,428	1,898,622

Wealth Holdings in 1850 (continued)

State: North Carolina

County	Male Slaves	Female Slaves	Slave Totals	Land
Alamance	741,820	624,145	1,365,965	959,359
Alexander	122,332	110,320	232,652	267,469
Alleghany*				
Anson	1,579,844	1,358,906	2,938,750	1,291,766
Ashe	139,468	117,806	257,274	484,958
Beaufort	1,282,344	966,482	2,248,826	606,061
Bertie	1,656,956	1,395,548	3,052,504	1,194,282
Bladen	1,036,252	829,370	1,865,622	828,556
Brunswick	874,888	553,964	1,428,852	527,549
Buncombe	402,696	337,264	739,960	1,275,287
Burke	525,980	397,546	923,526	573,657
Cabarras	653,075	518,215	1,171,290	897,317
Caldwell	267,036	242,310	509,346	432,068
Camden	547,400	388,090	935,490	967,795

Wealth Holdings in 1850   (continued)

State: North Carolina

County	Male Slaves	Female Slaves	Slave Totals	Land
Carteret	363,664	327,414	691,078	153,154
Caswell	1,849,260	1,485,380	3,334,640	1,403,624
Catawaba	354,428	314,018	672,446	893,424
Chatham	1,394,680	1,168,604	2,563,284	1,481,655
Cherokee	73,780	70,526	144,306	389,634
Chowan	884,884	689,894	1,574,778	799,690
Cleveland	405,076	347,902	752,978	558,584
Columbus	322,740	290,780	613,520	300,606
Craven	1,318,044	1,211,550	2,529,594	766,964
Cumberland	1,713,600	1,384,122	3,097,722	1,300,060
Currituck	591,668	461,768	1,053,436	728,065
Davidson	706,384	575,634	1,282,018	1,165,682
Davie	487,424	435,764	923,188	494,631
Duplin	1,402,772	1,166,240	2,569,012	1,402,489

Wealth Holdings in 1850   (continued)

State: North Carolina

County	Male Slaves	Female Slaves	Slave Totals	Land
Edgecomb	2,019,129	1,635,494	3,654,686	2,003,553
Forsythe	326,536	252,160	578,696	624,260
Franklin	1,282,344	1,064,982	2,347,326	841,750
Gaston	520,060	404,140	924,200	691,022
Gates	885,360	752,540	1,637,900	702,092
Granville	2,294,320	1,912,082	4,206,402	1,423,414
Greene	745,892	641,038	1,386,930	752,613
Guilford	736,372	628,824	1,365,196	1,500,574
Halifax	2,064,888	1,759,998	3,824,886	1,535,343
Harnet*				
Haywood	96,628	83,134	179,762	470,057

*   = did not exist in 1850
**   = did not exist in 1860
***   = no record

Wealth Holdings in 1850 (continued)

State: North Carolina

County	Male Slaves	Female Slaves	Slave Totals	Land
Henderson	225,148	172,966	398,114	380,876
Hertford	880,600	700,926	1,581,526	614,683
Hyde	646,408	479,104	1,125,512	1,112,799
Iredell	937,490	795,880	1,733,370	1,172,450
Jackson*				
Johnson	1,120,980	880,590	2,001,570	1,036,575
Jones	644,980	2,001,570	1,036,575	464,845
Lenior	975,324	792,334	1,767,658	1,166,525
Lihlington*				
Lincoln	509,796	378,240	888,036	727,428
Macon	122,808	111,502	234,310	385,341
Madison*				
Martin	819,196	623,702	1,442,898	731,986
Mc Dowell	287,504	253,342	540,846	560,015

Wealth Holdings in 1850   (continued)

State: North Carolina

County	Male Slaves	Female Slaves	Slave Totals	Land
Mecklenburg	1,258,544	1,083,894	2,342,438	1,210,933
Montgomery	394,128	357,752	751,880	386,269
Moore	440,745	392,170	832,915	479,242
Nash	931,056	797,850	1,728,906	640,859
New Hanover	2,077,740	1,608,308	3,686,048	994,439
North Hampton	1,568,896	1,197,760	2,755,545	1,055,479
Onslow	653,072	605,578	1,258,650	536,906
Orange	1,177,148	1,051,980	2,229,128	1,152,778
Pasquotank	775,404	640,250	1,416,654	1,213,390
Perquimans	800,632	600,062	1,400,694	1,023,792
Person	1,148,112	952,209	2,100,410	837,581
Pitt	1,584,604	1,288,774	2,873,378	1,109,425
Polk*				
Randolph	403,345	337,620	740,965	1,075,746

Wealth Holdings in 1850   (continued)

State: North Carolina

County	Male Slaves	Female Slaves	Slave Totals	Land
Richmond	1,108,128	919,596	2,027,724	630,154
Robeson	1,007,216	800,196	1,887,412	1,141,266
Rockingham	1,240,456	1,055,920	2,246,376	999,036
Rowan	889,644	761,602	1,651,246	1,110,175
Rutherford	697,816	551,206	1,249,022	993,621
Sampson	1,342,320	1,103,594	2,445,914	1,792,871
Stanly	351,288	261,616	612,904	356,774
Stokes	392,700	366,814	759,514	759,514
Surry	450,296	402,668	852,964	999,043
Tyrrel	428,850	308,025	736,875	322,120
Union	460,768	387,302	848,070	751,185
Wake	1,982,540	1,868,742	3,851,282	1,613,434
Waranga (Watauga)	30,464	25,216	55,680	350,937
Warren	2,072,504	1,698,140	3,770,644	1,267,424

Wealth Holdings in 1850 (continued)

State: North Carolina

County	Male Slaves	Female Slaves	Slave Totals	Land
Washington	526,932	416,458	943,390	389,433
Wayne	1,184,288	965,694	2,149,982	1,598,507
Wilkes	263,228	228,914	492,142	811,977
Wilson *				
Yancey	68,544	78,800	147,344	605,196

State: South Carolina

County	Male Slaves	Female Slaves	Slave Totals	Land
Abbeville	4,438,580	3,841,165	8,279,745	4,806,236
Anderson	1,712,546	1,537,272	3,249,818	2,457,104
Barnwell	3,313,268	2,758,536	6,071,804	2,762,644
Beaufort	7,083,954	6,202,548	13,286,502	5,377,296
Charleston	9,741,220	9,136,908	18,878,128	5,667,091
Chester	2,318,420	1,974,060	4,292,48-	3,044,911

Wealth Holdings in 1850 (continued)

State: South Carolina

County	Male Slaves	Female Slaves	Slave Totals	Land
Chesterfield	917,200	776,770	1,693,970	867,338
Clarenon*				
Colleton	7,161,556	6,363,324	13,524,880	3,482,433
Darlington	2,359,390	1,977,624	4,337,014	2,818,445
Edgefield	5,407,076	4,447,872	9,854,948	5,427,872
Fairfield	3,374,000	2,814,768	6,188,768	3,157,980
Georgetown	4,198,702	3,752,100	7,950,802	5,476,723
Greenville	1,552,165	1,375,755	2,751,510	2,017,956
Horry	494,532	402,336	896,868	370,406
Kershaw	2,249,012	1,861,596	4,110,608	1,386,113
Lancaster	1,198,734	979,308	2,178,042	1,505,833
Laurens	2,872,238	2,329,272	5,201,610	3,898,463
Lexington	1,295,125	1,101,672	2,306,806	1,032,305
Marion	1,701,240	1,524,985	3,226,225	2,573,322

Wealth Holdings in 1850   (continued)

State: South Carolina

County	Male Slaves	Female Slaves	Slave Totals	Land
Marlborough	1,305,256	1,104,840	2,410,096	1,908,108
Newberry	3,014,438	2,509,452	5,523,880	3,555,320
Orangeburgh	3,537,309	3,091,572	6,628,970	3,049,734
Pickens	844,946	743,292	1,588,238	1,640,290
Richland	3,062,628	2,553,408	5,616,036	1,992,050
Spartanburgh	1,975,730	1,540,050	3,515,780	2,680,921
Sumter	5,357,746	4,574,592	9,950,338	3,599,102
Union	2,438,920	2,084,544	4,523,464	3,036,198
Williamsburgh	1,981,020	1,700,028	3,681,048	827,076
York	1,941,014	1,538,460	3,479,474	2,686,934

State: Tennessee

County	Male Slaves	Female Slaves	Slave Totals	Land
Anderson	147,080	148,047	295,127	489,482

Wealth Holdings in 1850 (continued)

State: Tennessee

County	Male Slaves	Female Slaves	Slave Totals	Land
Bedford	1,786,142	1,529,550	3,315,692	2,298,570
Benton	115,083	103,950	219,033	356,148
Bledsoe	294,101	213,400	507,501	551,839
Blount	347,268	307,450	654,718	1,168,913
Bradley	240,934	210,100	451,034	1,037,435
Campbell	180,277	90,750	191,027	390,132
Cannon	257,086	244,750	501,836	686,146
Carroll	992,002	902,000	1,894,022	1,008,637
Carter	111,045	265,100	376,145	426,111
Cheatham*				
Clairborne	231,512	172,150	403,662	697,284

*   = did not exist in 1850
**   = did not exist in 1860
*** = no records

Wealth Holdings in 1850   (continued)

State: <u>Tennessee</u>

<u>County</u>	<u>Male Slaves</u>	<u>Female Slaves</u>	<u>Slave Totals</u>	<u>Land</u>
Cocke	242,834	191,931	434,768	733,239
Coffee	409,857	356,400	766,257	549,987
Cumberland*				
Davidson	4,798,490	3,798,300	8,496,790	6,420,623
Decatur	253,048	189,200	442,248	311,180
De Kalb	203,246	196,900	400,146	488,777
Dickson	754,433	542,850	1,297,283	449,497
Dyer	487,252	402,050	889,302	696,698
Fayette	5,058,268	4,191,000	9,249,268	3,404,217
Fentress	50,475	40,150	90,625	224,069
Franklin	1,224,187	971,850	2,196,037	1,417,482
Gibson	1,331,194	1,199,000	2,530,194	2,155,846
Giles	2,023,087	2,653,674	5,676,761	4,466,028
Grainger	365,439	261,800	627,239	818,781

Wealth Holdings in 1850   (continued)

State: Tennessee

County	Male Slaves	Female Slaves	Slave Totals	Land
Greene	353,998	194,700	548,698	1,656,083
Grundy	74,703	65,450	140,153	183,463
Hamilton	205,938	198,550	404,488	923,649
Hancock	72,684	41,700	124,384	424,055
Hardeman	2,380,401	1,940,400	4,320,801	1,737,957
Hardin	421,971	337,150	759,121	568,568
Hawkins	550,514	473,000	1,023,514	1,358,773
Haywood	2,846,790	2,304,500	5,151,290	1,763,335
Henderson	829,136	739,750	1,568,886	738,701
Henry	1,571,455	1,353,000	2,924,455	1,222,571
Hickman	638,999	494,084	1,133,083	780,819
Humphreys	343,903	317,900	661,803	384,775
Jackson	545,803	317,900	948,403	855,076
Jefferson	521,575	463,100	984,675	1,343,056

Wealth Holdings in 1850 (continued)

State: Tennessee

County	Male Slaves	Female Slaves	Slave Totals	Land
Johnson	70,665	52,250	122,915	323,286
Knox	732,897	589,600	1,322,497	1,917,853
Lauderdale	582,818	485,650	1,068,468	458,829
Lawrence	380,918	320,650	701,568	681,472
Lewis	222,763	216,150	438,913	402,116
Lincoln	1,846,712	1,548,250	3,394,962	3,372,294
Macon	246,991	221,100	468,091	425,148
Mc Minn	492,444	459,221	951,665	1.325,875
Mc Nairy	448,891	396,000	844,891	798,147
Madison	2,769,395	2,398,000	5,167,395	2,262,294
Marion	187,767	149,600	337,367	660,182
Marshall	1,169,674	1,014,200	2,183,874	2,033,392
Maury	4,119,433	3,518,350	7,637,783	4,228,008
Meigs	127,870	112,750	240,620	130,723

Wealth Holdings in 1850   (continued)

State: Tennessee

County	Male Slaves	Female Slaves	Slave Totals	Land
Monroe	380,245	337,700	717,945	1,303,637
Montgomery	3,077,629	2,350,150	5,427,779	1,319,041
Morgan	30,958	30,250	61,208	323,951
Obion	359,664	299,650	659,314	647,414
Overton	337,173	304,156	641,323	690,000
Perry	99,604	90,280	189,804	429,043
Polk	127,870	113,300	241,170	588,109
Putnam *				
Rhea	139,984	124,850	264,834	368,083
Roane	610,134	420,750	930,884	1,030,078
Robertson	1,512,904	1,264,456	2,777,354	1,350,911
Rutherford	3,891,959	3,333,556	7,225,509	4,386,722
Scott	11,441	11,000	22,441	97,670
Sequatchie *				

Wealth Holdings in 1850 (continued)

State: Tennessee

County	Male Slaves	Female Slaves	Slave Totals	Land
Sevier	125,851	113,850	239,701	486,493
Shelby	4,809,258	3,891,250	8,700,508	3,320,752
Smith	1,515,397	1,208,655	2,724,052	1,242,010
Stewart	1,050,553	551,100	1,601,653	363,545
Sullivan	349,960	260,156	610,110	1,361,449
Sumner	2,644,216	2,193,400	4,837,617	2,748,236
Tipton	1,407,916	1,128,600	2,536,516	1,074,807
Union*				
Van Buren	56,532	49,600	106,032	143,679
Warren	563,301	470,800	1,034,101	709,680
Washington	311,599	253,550	565,149	1,747,869

* = did not exist in 1850
** = did not exist in 1860
*** = no records

Wealth Holdings in 1850   (continued)

State: Tennessee

County	Male Slaves	Female Slaves	Slave Totals	Land
Wayne	322,367	246,400	458,767	547,053
Weakley	1,008,827	848,650	1,857,477	846,002
White	388,321	344,300	732,621	772,197
Williamson	4,233,843	3,540,900	7,774,743	5,221,232
Wilson	2,309,987	1,998,450	4,307,537	2,794,885

State: Texas

County	Male Slaves	Female Slaves	Slave Totals	Land
Anderson	211,423	181,127	392,550	222,577
Angelina	69,201	56,551	125,752	134,669
Atacosa *				
Austin	555,006	432,586	978,592	
Banderah *				
Bastrop	307,560	277,508	585,068	207,281

177

Wealth Holdings in 1850 (continued)

State: Texas

County	Male Slaves	Female Slaves	Slave Totals	Land
Bee *				
Bell *				
Bexar	120,927	124,179	245,106	210,868
Blanco *				
Bosque *				
Bowie	545,919	494,384	1,040,303	198,153
Brazoria	1,243,521	1,001,011	2,244,532	1,050,421
Brazos	50,328	44,309	94,636	64,847
Buchanan *				
Burleson	183,138	138,171	321,309	147,190
Burnet *				
Caldwell	89,472	84,635	174,007	67,287
Calhoun	87,924	61,738	149,662	71,937
Cameron	16,776	16,907	33,683	98,446

Wealth Holdings in 1850   (continued)

State: Texas

County	Male Slaves	Female Slaves	Slave Totals	Land
Comanche*				
Cass	663,351	548,020	1,211,371	502,092
Chambers*				
Cherokee	417,303	397,606	814,909	549,430
Collin	46,134	39,644	85,778	164,840
Colorado	242,553	218,042	460,595	187,614
Comal	21,669	16,907	38,576	76,295
Cook	699	--	699	60,113
Coryell*				
Dallas	64,308	66,462	130,770	164,972
Denton	3,495	2,915	6,410	20,203
Dewitt	186,790	161,777	348,567	185,126
Ellis	26,562	22,154	48,716	61,309
El Paso*				

Wealth Holdings in 1850   (continued)

State: Texas

County	Male Slaves	Female Slaves	Slave Totals	Land
Erath*				
Falls*				
Fannin	171,954	162,074	334,028	282,100
Fayette	334,821	308,990	643,811	293,881
Fort Bend	536,832	452,991	989,823	344,048
Freestone*				
Frio*				
Galveston	228,573	225,038	453,611	33,088
Gillespie	1,398	1,749	3,147	24,805
Goliad	76,191	60,632	136,823	52,286
Gonzales	199,819	184,987	384,797	493,084
Guadalupe	118,830	95,612	21,442	199,049
Grayson	64,308	54,802	119,110	163,367
Grimes	592,752	478,643	1,071,395	276,296

Wealth Holdings in 1850 (continued)

State: Texas

County	Male Slaves	Female Slaves	Slave Totals	Land
Hamilton*				
Hardin*				
Harris	280,299	290,917	571,216	129,661
Harrison	2,076,030	1,867,932	3,943,962	1,056,116
Hays	41,940	38,478	80,418	55,223
Henderson	29,358	22,737	42,095	60,361
Hidalgo*				
Hill*				
Hopkins	44,736	51,887	96,623	107,480
Houston	229,971	198,220	428,191	174,739
Hunt	13,281	12,826	26,107	36,849

*   = did not exist in 1850
**   = did not exist in 1860
***   = no records

Wealth Holdings in 1850   (continued)

State: Texas

County	Male Slaves	Female Slaves	Slave Totals	Land
Jack*				
Jackson	119,358	95,139	214,497	165,885
Jasper	186,633	158,576	345,209	301,120
Jefferson	93,666	78,705	172,371	49,741
Johnson*				
Karnes*				
Kaufman	22,368	19,239	41,607	82,788
Kerr*				
Lamar	381,654	310,739	692,393	474,219
Lampasa*				
Lavaca	139,101	134,090	273,191	158,986
Leon	231,369	171,402	402,771	194,554
Liberty	299,172	263,476	562,588	234,333
Limestone	199,215	192,973	392,188	118,306

Wealth Holdings in 1850   (continued)

State: Texas

County	Male Slaves	Female Slaves	Slave Totals	Land
Live Oak *				
Llano *				
Mc Lennan *				
Madison *				
Marion *				
Mason *				
Matagorda	455,748	321,816	777,564	472,823
Maveric *				
Medina	7,771	5,580	13,351	20,306
Milam	146,091	131,175	277,266	165,365
Montague *				
Montgomery	339,714	267,014	606,728	192,182
Nacogdoches	472,524	420,343	892,867	279,009
Navarro	87,375	70,543	147,918	123,446

Wealth Holdings in 1850   (continued)

State: Texas

County	Male Slaves	Female Slaves	Slave Totals	Land
Newton	146,790	124,179	270,969	160,231
Nueces	13,281	16,324	29,605	103,769
Orange*				
Palo Pinto*				
Panola	404,022	355,630	759,652	211,976
Parker*				
Polk	250,941	257,103	508,044	476,281
Presidio*				
Red River	489,171	404,129	893,300	326,891
Refugio	4,194	7,579	11,773	19,284
Robertson	93,666	74,041	167,707	57,519
Rusk	768,900	599,907	1,368,807	647,750
Sabine	332,025	267,014	599,039	392,393
San Augustine	531,240	465,234	996,474	243,023

Wealth Holdings in 1850   (continued)

State: Texas

County	Male Slaves	Female Slaves	Slave Totals	Land
San Patricio	699	1,166	1,865	22,779
San Saba*				
Shackleford*				
Shelby	323,637	289,168	612,805	420,014
Smith	233,466	222,123	455,589	269,946
Starr*				
Tarrant	25,164	16,907	42,071	21,390
Titus	157,275	139,920	297,195	171,407
Travis	287,506	232,534	520,040	292,268
Trinity*				
Tyler	136,305	128,260	264,565	136,820
Upshur	230,670	202,884	433,554	250,124
Uvalde*				
Van Zandt	13,281	12,243	25,524	74,208

Wealth Holdings in 1850 (continued)

State: Texas

County	Male Slaves	Female Slaves	Slave Totals	Land
Victoria	218,787	147,499	366,286	200,911
Walker	449,457	379,533	828,990	416,817
Washington	982,095	812,702	1,794,797	651,383
Webb	16,776	16,907	33,683	98,446
Wharton	438,972	353,298	792,270	300,791
Williamson	45,435	52,470	97,905	261,985
Wise *				
Wood *				
Young *				

State: Virginia

County	Male Slaves	Female Slaves	Slave Totals	Land
Accomack	1,215,575	938,475	2,154,050	3,769,345
Albemarle	3,270,720	2,429,268	5,699,988	5,380,230

Wealth Holdings in 1850 (continued)

State: Virginia

County	Male Slaves	Female Slaves	Slave Totals	Land
Alexandria	266,400	314,280	580,680	417,152
Alleghany	182,400	120,668	303,068	524,681
Amelia	1,633,440	1,280,012	2,913,452	1,436,506
Amherst	1,400,160	1,122,872	2,523,032	1,853,021
Appomattox	1,140,960	906,756	2,047,710	1,030,737
Augusta	1,258,560	913,352	2,171,912	7,118,139
Barbour	25,920	22,892	48,812	1,753,056
Bath	237,600	154,812	392,412	698,545
Bedford	2,493,600	1,814,288	4,307,888	3,267,078
Berkeley	483,295	402,525	885,820	3,641,303
Boone	47,040	31,816	78,856	258,056

*   = did not exist in 1850
**   = did not exist in 1860
*** = no records

Wealth Holdings in 1850   (continued)

State: Virginia

County	Male Slaves	Female Slaves	Slave Totals	Land
Botecourt	960,960	651,452	1,612,412	1,837,714
Braxton	19,680	17,848	37,528	1,289,006
Brooke	7,680	5,432	13,112	1,290,259
Brunswick	1,998,720	1,593,128	3,591,848	1,074,989
Buchanan *				
Buckingham	1,951,200	1,523,288	3,474,488	2,021,888
Cabell	91,200	76,824	168,024	749,211
Calhoun *				
Campbell	2,694,240	2,038,940	4,733,180	2,403,552
Caroline	2,376,960	2,127,792	4,504,752	2,730,718
Carrol	31,200	34,532	65,732	505,446
Charles City	696,895	469,320	1,166,215	896,382
Charlotte	2,164,800	1,671,116	3,835,916	2,500,752
Chesterfield	2,217,600	1,486,040	3,703,640	1,581,040

Wealth Holdings in 1850   (continued)

State: Virginia

County	Male Slaves	Female Slaves	Slave Totals	Land
Clarke	888,000	652,616	1,540,616	3,128,095
Clay*				
Craig*				
Culpepper	1,624,800	1,313,380	2,938,180	2,941,467
Cumberland	1,546,560	1,150,420	2,696,980	1,525,397
Dinwiddie	1,611,680	2,011,004	4,622,684	1,474,958
Doddridge	8,160	5,432	13,592	275,981
Elizabeth City	508,320	405,072	913,392	663,287
Essex	1,645,440	1,247,032	2,892,472	1,903,031
Fairfax	756,480	620,412	1,376,892	2,298,413
Fauquier	2,365,060	1,930,020	4,295,080	6,025,819
Fayette	35,040	30,652	65,602	495,871
Floyd	94,560	89,628	184,548	593,103
Fluvanna	1,163,520	853,988	2,017,508	1,402,435

Wealth Holdings in 1850   (continued)

State: Virginia

County	Male Slaves	Female Slaves	Slave Totals	Land
Franklin	1,306,080	1,139,168	2,445,248	1,671,153
Frederick	431,840	443,872	974,712	3,825,143
Giles	156,960	126,488	283,448	864,378
Gilmer	18,720	12,804	31,524	303,691
Gloucester	1,308,480	1,051,480	2,359,960	1,547,806
Goochland	1,451,520	1,044,108	2,495,628	2,052,973
Grayson	124,155	93,105	217,260	592,436
Greenbrier	305,280	257,632	562,912	10,526
Greene	391,680	328,248	719,928	13,463
Greenville	897,600	712,368	1,609,968	418,629
Halifax	3,503,520	2,686,512	6,190,032	3,352,570
Hampshire	333,120	276,644	609,764	3,037,670
Hancock	--	1,164	1,164	1,157,882
Hanover	1,988,160	1,579,548	3,567,708	2,048,620

Wealth Holdings in 1850   (continued)

State: Virginia

County	Male Slaves	Female Slaves	Slave Totals	Land
Haroy	305,280	234,352	539,632	2,575,891
Harrison	108,000	99,716	207,716	2,193,182
Henrico	4,029,120	2,881,288	6,910,408	115,761
Henry	730,955	652,425	1,383,380	803,669
Highland	89,760	66,348	156,108	1,231,995
Isle of Wright	801,120	627,396	1,428,516	963,084
Jackson	10,560	11,640	22,200	848,932
James City	443,520	355,020	798,540	550,692
Jefferson	1,037,760	814,800	1,852,560	5,284,817
Kanawha	910,080	477,240	1,387,320	1,048,528
King & Queen	1,315,200	1,126,752	2,441,952	1,293,201
King George	816,000	633,992	1,449,992	1,094,852
King William	1,316,640	1,138,004	2,454,644	1,467,878
Lancaster	608,160	531,948	1,140,108	687,959

Wealth Holdings in 1850 (continued)

State: Virginia

County	Male Slaves	Female Slaves	Slave Totals	Land
Lee	183,500	169,630	353,130	1,110,759
Lewis	82,080	76,436	158,516	1,143,408
Logan	21,600	16,296	37,896	277,306
Loudon	1,298,400	1,091,444	2,389,844	8,374,262
Louisa	2,298,720	1,890,724	4,189,444	2,576,057
Lunenburg	1,686,240	1,361,104	3,047,344	1,041,334
Madison	1,124,640	890,072	2,014,712	2,127,421
Marion	19,680	19,788	39,468	1,613,843
Marshall	13,440	8,148	21,588	1,661,475
Mason	149,280	127,264	276,544	1,284,840
Mathews	682,560	555,616	1,238,176	625,951

*   = did not exist in 1850
**   = did not exist in 1860
***   = no records

Wealth Holdings in 1850   (continued)

State: Virginia

County	Male Slaves	Female Slaves	Slave Totals	Land
Meckleburgh	3,072,380	2,279,130	5,351,510	2,484,915
Mercer	43,680	36,860	80,540	392,464
Middlesex	564,480	429,128	993,608	887,300
Monongalia	35,040	38,024	73,064	1,587,924
Monroe	264,000	195,164	459,164	2,058,327
Montgomery	338,880	283,628	622,508	1,569,208
Morgan	27,360	25,609	52,968	459,528
Nansemond	1,150,560	856,316	2,015,876	1,682,748
Nelson	1,450,080	1,163,612	2,613,692	1,924,438
New Kent	804,000	642,916	1,446,916	746,364
Nicholas	17,745	15,100	32,845	367,083
Norfolk	2,277,600	2,115,764	4,392,364	1,226,990
North Hampton	846,240	629,192	1,538,820	235,877
Northumberland	913,440	692,580	1,606,020	941,296

Wealth Holdings in 1850   (continued)

State: Virginia

County	Male Slaves	Female Slaves	Slave Totals	Land
Nottoway	1,438,560	1,138,780	2,577,340	1,136,137
Ohio	29,760	37,636	67,396	1,985,432
Orange	1,445,760	1,076,700	2,522,460	1,875,802
Page	241,440	171,884	413,324	1,784,040
Patrick	521,280	466,376	987,656	720,075
Pendleton	81,120	58,200	139,320	1,054,589
Pittsylvania	3,094,560	2,390,856	5,485,416	2,793,890
Pleasants*				
Pocahontas	65,895	55,000	120,895	927,699
Powhatan	1,305,600	947,496	2,373,991	1,409,076
Preston	18,720	18,624	37,344	1,140,530
Prince Edward	1,776,000	1,304,068	3,080,068	1,577,129
Prince George	1,084,320	801,220	1,885,540	1,151,523
Prince William	583,200	473,360	1,056,560	1,469,888

Wealth Holdings in 1850 (continued)

State: Virginia

County	Male Slaves	Female Slaves	Slave Totals	Land
Princess Ann	786,240	556,780	1,343,020	1,088,459
Pulaski	388,320	250,648	638,968	1,158,997
Putnam	139,680	128,040	267,720	495,964
Raleigh	4,320	4,656	8,976	154,697
Randolph	45,600	41,128	86,728	856,278
Rappahannock	915,680	738,535	1,654,215	2,081,158
Richmond	528,000	429,128	957,128	573,826
Ritchie	1,920	4,268	6,188	455,145
Roane *				
Roanoke	620,160	456,288	1,076,448	1,740,138
Rockbridge	1,111,200	710,040	1,821,240	3,240,248
Rockingham	579,840	424,472	1,004,312	5,941,402
Russell	229,920	191,672	421,592	1,102,406

Wealth Holdings in 1850   (continued)

State: Virginia

County	Male Slaves	Female Slaves	Slave Totals	Land
Scott	109,440	91,180	200,620	713,257
Shenandoah	228,000	165,288	393,288	3,088,462
Smythe	263,520	194,776	458,296	1,595,903
South Hampton	1,394,880	1,025,872	2,420,752	1.046,741
Spottsylvania	1,708,455	1,474,735	3,183,190	1,265,675
Stafford	787,300	618,084	1,405,284	1,100,490
Surry	634,560	407,400	1,041,960	530,811
Sussex	1,474,080	1,089,504	2,563,584	588,094
Taylor	36,480	34,144	70,624	922,056
Tazewell	252,000	204,476	456,476	1,198,334
Tucker*				
Tyler	6,720	8,924	15,644	608,325
Upshur*				
Warwick	229,920	160,632	390,552	252,945

Wealth Holdings in 1850   (continued)

State: Virginia

County	Male Slaves	Female Slaves	Slave Totals	Land
Warren	419,040	331,352	750,392	1,514,287
Washington	515,520	402,744	918,264	1,977,354
Wayne	37,920	42,292	80,212	615,815
Webster *				
Westmoreland	812,000	674,620	1,486,620	1,109,553
Wetzel	2,880	4,268	7,148	498,891
Wirt	7,200	6,506	13,796	402,943
Wise *				
Wood	83,040	75,660	158,700	1,325,356
Wyoming	14,400	12,028	26,428	118,404
Wythe	552,000	387,224	939,224	2,137,095
York	523,200	407,400	930,600	703,524

Wealth Holdings in 1860, in Dollars

State: Alabama

County	Male Slaves	Female Slaves	Slave Totals	Land
Augusta	5,292,401	6,164,039	11,456,440	2,901,285
Baldwin	2,530,089	1,363,264	3,893,353	468,090
Barbour	8,951,841	7,607,872	16,649,713	4,960,812
Benton **				
Bibb	2,129,294	1,837,360	3,966,654	1,442,455
Blount	333,055	347,480	680,535	832,500
Butler	3,919,957	3,177,582	7,097,539	2,950,744
Calhoun	2,360,739	2,106,776	4,467,515	2,709,394
Chambers	6,603,521	5,611,088	12,214,609	3,035,933
Cherokee	1,656,243	1,431,808	3,088,051	2,979,265
Choctaw	3,096,499	3,348,184	7,334,683	2,746,406

*   = did not exist in 1850
**   = did not exist in 1860
*** = no reocrds

Wealth Holdings in 1860 (continued)

State: Alabama

County	Male Slaves	Female Slaves	Slave Totals	Land
Clarke	4,041,016	3,425,667	7,466,683	3,255,548
Coffee	749,656	687,816	1,437,472	1,004,062
Conecuh	2,757,018	2,279,088	5,036,106	1,045,700
Coosa	2,839,435	2,540,888	5,380,323	1,672,376
Covington	442,568	413,168	855,736	538,155
Dale	924,781	849,265	1,774,046	1,431,122
Dallas	14,411,685	12,098,016	26,509,701	9,311,714
De Kalb	483,212	396,032	879,244	1,100,609
Fayette	908,845	835,856	1,744,701	739,641
Franklin	4,633,416	4,109,784	8,743,200	4,096,733
Greene	12,809,217	10,682,766	23,491,983	9,176,802
Hancock **				
Henry	2,481,542	2,092,496	4,574,038	2,154,860
Jackson	1,933,977	1,582,224	3,516,201	3,121,085

Wealth Holdings in 1860   (continued)

State: Alabama

County	Male Slaves	Female Slaves	Slave Totals	Land
Jefferson	1,450,765	1,282,344	2,733,109	1,219,865
Lauderdale	3,770,860	3,180,632	6,951,492	4,554,063
Lawrence	3,661,839	3,134,036	6,795,875	2,996,285
Limestone	4,325,199	3,874,640	8,199,839	3,592,495
Lowndes	10,787,595	9,143,960	19,931,555	9,040,470
Macon	10,118,098	8,652,728	18,770,826	5,825,099
Madison	6,801,088	6,879,152	13,680,240	6,078,806
Marengo	13,800,961	11,011,293	24,812,254	10,291,862
Marion	609,280	596,904	1,193,808	729,765
Marshall	1,000,294	867,272	1,867,566	1,372,766
Mobile	6,592,231	5,138,896	11,731,127	1,186,763
Monroe	4,817,443	4,146,008	8,062,451	2,672,000
Montgomery	13,604,992	10,958,246	24,563,238	9,883,964
Morgan	1,346,897	1,775,480	2,122,377	1,441,964

Wealth Holdings in 1860   (continued)

State: Alabama

County	Male Slaves	Female Slaves	Slave Totals	Land
Perry	10,393,574	8,448,048	18,841,622	7,257,412
Pickens	6,688,196	5,866,224	12,554,420	4,016,618
Pike	4,963,084	4,102,168	9,065,252	3,744,687
Randolph	928,561	917,821	1,846,382	1,950,170
Russell	8,757,653	7,369,432	16,127,085	4,959,649
St. Clair	973,198	842,040	1,825,238	1,370,662
Shelby	2,070,586	1,101,464	3,152,060	1,401,230
Sumter	10,532,441	8,205,240	18,738,681	5,303,979
Tauadega	5,011,638	4,053,828	8,107,656	3,111,205
Tauapoosa	3,615,058	3,270,120	6,885,178	3,256,377
Tuscaloosa	5,803,060	4,657,184	10,460,244	5,025,157
Walker	327,410	258,944	586,354	613,820
Washington	1,442,862	1,128,120	3,570,982	791,710
Wilcox	10,141,466	8,347,061	18,488,527	7,311,117

Wealth Holdings in 1860   (continued)

State: __Alabama__

County	Male Slaves	Female Slaves	Slave Totals	Land
Winston	10,141,466	8,347,061	18,488,527	7,311,117
State: __Arkansas__				
Arkansas	3,111,318	2,155,278	5,266,596	5,498,395
Ashley	2,087,085	1,810,224	3,897,309	2,532,356
Benton	210,210	208,728	418,938	1,411,920
Bradley	1,451,835	1,450,800	2,902,635	2,084,198
Calhoun	565,950	453,960	1,019,910	499,136
Carroll	159,645	168,359	336,718	836,970
Chicot	4,469,850	3,370,536	7,840,386	4,399,554
Clark	1,242,780	1,050,192	2,292,972	1,254,607
Columbia	2,089,395	1,662,336	2,486,259	2,041,073
Conway	435,435	396,864	832,299	923,263
Craighead	50,820	40,248	91,068	268,982

Wealth Holdings in 1860   (continued)

State: Arkansas

County	Male Slaves	Female Slaves	Slave Totals	Land
Crawford	453,065	418,275	871,340	615,073
Crittenden	1,417,185	1,037,088	2,454,273	2,408,415
Dallas	2,140,215	1,509,768	3,649,983	75,500
Desha	2,248,785	1,700,712	3,949,497	128,064
Drew	1,977,188	1,652,316	3,629,504	67,024
Franklin	569,415	499,824	1,069,239	42,288
Fulton	38,115	51,480	89,595	25,268
Greene	172,771	575,574		
Hempstead	3,142,755	2,481,336	5,624,091	2,029,418
Hot Springs	334,230	290,642	624,882	797,525
Independence	741,510	639,288	1,380,798	1,695,951

*   = did not exist in 1850
**   = did not exist in 1860
***   = no records

203

Wealth Holdings in 1860 (continued)

State: Arkansas

County	Male Slaves	Female Slaves	Slave Totals	Land
Izard	209,055	188,136	395,191	750,076
Jackson	1,442,595	1,208,376	2,650,971	2,063,231
Jefferson	4,214,595	3,239,496	7,454,091	6,952,596
Johnson	533,341	443,546	976,887	947,409
LaFayette	2,632,245	1,872,936	4,505,181	2,356,283
Lawrence	292,215	229,320	521,535	1,089,470
Madison	154,770	151,632	306,402	757,783
Marion	136,290	133,848	270,138	462,956
Mississippi	817,811	682,471	1,500,382	1,741,201
Monroe	1,308,615	1,008,072	2,316,687	1,458,212
Montgomery	55,440	41,184	96,624	294,250
Newton	13,860	11,232	25,092	190,491
Ouachita	2,515,590	2,132,208	4,647,798	1,988,237
Perry	178,403	139,985	318,388	422,441

Wealth Holdings in 1860   (continued)

State: <u>Arkansas</u>

<u>County</u>	<u>Male Slaves</u>	<u>Female Slaves</u>	<u>Slave Totals</u>	<u>Land</u>
Phillips	5,260,355	3,965,832	9,326,187	8,037,268
Pike	130,515	104,832	235,347	439,436
Poinsett	597,135	524,160	1,121,295	912,217
Polk	88,935	88,920	177,855	297,360
Pope	545,203	329,555	984,758	1,032,383
Praire	1,623,930	1,329,120	2,053,050	2,051,830
Pulaski	2,047,815	1,536,912	3,584,727	3,361,692
Randolph	199,815	171,288	371,103	71,102
St. Francis	1,522,290	1,207,440	2,729,730	2,498,918
Saline	381,366	358,845	740,211	690,206
Scott	125,895	99,216	225,111	520,782
Searcy	56,595	41,184	97,779	318,198
Sebastian	356,895	343,512	700,407	956,068
Sevier	1,966,965	1,530,360	3,497,325	2,284,692

Wealth Holdings in 1860   (continued)

State: Arkansas

County	Male Slaves	Female Slaves	Slave Totals	Land
Union	3,659.246	2,978,237	6,637,483	2,089,904
Van Buren	107,415	100,152	207,567	506,147
Washington	853,545	701,064	1,554,609	2,010,927
White	791,175	602,640	1,483,815	1,193,912
Yell	602,910	443,664	1,046,474	1,201,951

State: Florida

County	Male Slaves	Female Slaves	Slave Totals	Land
Alachua	2,526,319	2,096,688	4,623,007	1,403,602
Benton**				
Brevard	13,164	12,129	25,293	23,340
Calhoun	275,347	250,044	525,391	218,540
Clay	291,802	233,250	525,052	126,880
Columbia	1,200,270	930,206	2,130,476	613,492
Dade	1,097	933	2,030	***

Wealth Holdings in 1860 (continued)

State: Florida

County	Male Slaves	Female Slaves	Slave Totals	Land
Duval	1,136,492	865,824	2,002,316	230,317
Escambia	1,141,977	813,576	1,955,553	28,875
Franklin	306,113	233,441	539,554	5,000
Gadsden	3,059,533	2,409,939	5,469,472	1,417,050
Hamilton	753,639	649,368	1,403,007	441,993
Hillsborough	281,642	269,102	550,744	178,670
Holmes	53,753	57,846	111,599	62,753
Jackson	2,036,091	2,262,525	5,198,616	1,366,189
Jefferson	3,334,880	3,050,910	6,385,790	1,646,074
Lafayette	320,877	257,835	578,712	179,090
Leon	4,006,837	4,135,056	9,131,891	2,482,211
Levy	193,072	157,677	350,749	84,017

* = did not exist in 1850
** = did not exist in 1860
*** = no record

Wealth Holdings in 1860   (continued)

State: Florida

County	Male Slaves	Female Slaves	Slave Totals	Land
Liberty	291,802	235,116	526,918	373,940
Madison	2,033,170	1,924,694	3,957,864	1,460,002
Manatex	139,319	109,161	248,480	97,095
Marion	2,031,184	2,420,202	5,351,386	1,887,115
Monroe	278,638	179,136	457,775	11,300
Nassau	971,493	689,209	1,660,702	145,455
New River	422,345	328,416	750,761	365,049
Orange	98,730	69,975	168,705	90,555
Putnam	592,380	467,433	1,059,813	210,800
Santa Rosa	1,049,498	485,779	1,535,277	23,285
St. Johns	483,777	501,021	984,798	69,530
Suwawnee	505,717	371,334	877,051	300,207
Sumter	298,384	271,910	550,294	199,873

Wealth Holdings in 1860   (continued)

State: Florida

County	Male Slaves	Female Slaves	Slave Totals	Land
Taylor	66,244	63,651	129,895	75,625
Volusia	93,245	137,151	230,396	99,810
Wakulla	620,902	545,805	1,166,707	287,339
Walton	242,437	201,528	443,965	154,671
Washington	239,280	210,472	449,752	86,983

State: Georgia

County	Male Slaves	Female Slaves	Slave Totals	Land
Appling	305,968	297,756	603,724	364,901
Baker	1,813,934	1,424,696	3,238,630	1,666,965
Baldwin	2,698,110	1,985,016	4,583,126	1,110,163
Banks	573,376	432,600	1,005,976	248,484
Berrien	205,530	192,816	398,346	474,950
Bibb	3,773,441	2,893,553	6,666,994	1,414,050
Brooks	1,677,986	1,369,488	3,047,456	1,486,140

Wealth Holdings in 1860   (continued)

State: Georgia

County	Male Slaves	Female Slaves	Slave Totals	Land
Bryan	1,208,938	967,376	2,176,314	524,561
Bullock	1,089,836	911,344	2,001,180	908,337
Burke	6,152,198	4,955,536	11,107,734	4,034,000
Butts	1,778,124	1,218,582	2,996,706	932,303
Calhoun	1,636,862	1,114,872	2,751,734	1,028,452
Camden	2,126,972	1,696,616	3,823,488	901,520
Campbell	989,706	869,320	1,859,026	1,255,086
Carroll	930,682	798,456	1,729,138	1,351,973
Cass	2,292,016	1,651,902	3,943,918	2,257,227
Catoosa	368,900	292,520	661,420	822,780
Charlton	396,204	146,672	542,976	61,955
Chatham	7,427,538	6,137,152	13,564,690	3,216,604
Chattahuechee	1,410,252	1,159,368	2,569,620	1,027,088
Chattooga	1,016,266	850,772	1,867,038	522,273

Wealth Holdings in 1860   (continued)

State: Georgia

County	Male Slaves	Female Slaves	Slave Totals	Land
Cherokee	593,402	514,176	1,107,578	1,358,284
Clark	2,822,612	2,374,768	5,197,380	1,949,806
Clay.	1,142,536	944,304	2,086,840	762,111
Clayton	562,260	519,229	1,081,489	660,807
Clinch	220,286	196,112	416,398	368,176
Cobb	1,984,682	1,566,424	3,551,106	1,533,869
Coffee	296,731	271,180	567,911	273,622
Colquit	55,862	47,792	103,654	137,187
Columbia	4,291,888	3,365,216	7,657,104	2,194,579
Coweta	3,624,706	3,087,528	6,712,234	2,613,497
Crawford	2,260,830	1,709,800	3,970,630	1,232,668

*   = did not exist in 1850
**   = did not exist in 1860
***   = no record

Wealth Holdings in 1860   (continued)

State: __Georgia__

County	Male Slaves	Female Slaves	Slave Totals	Land
Dade	161,262	114,536	275,709	415,160
Dawson	170,748	131,016	301,764	397,507
Decatur	3,026,397	2,394,963	5,421,360	2,205,996
De Kalb	1,012,894	819,056	1,831,950	929,906
Dooly	2,074,272	1,707,328	3,781,600	1,647,347
Dougherty	3,275,832	2,400,312	5,676,144	2,995,923
Early	2,157,538	1,576,312	3,733,850	1,544,969
Eckols	162,898	118,196	1,747,194	205,971
Effingham	1,154,130	846,248	2,000,378	696,413
Elbert	2,998,630	2,308,024	5,306,654	1,901,904
Emanuel	658,750	539,720	1,198,470	283,396
Fannin	80,104	55,208	135,312	366,968
Fayette	972,443	886,482	1,859,025	1,069,610
Floyd	3,053,438	2,443,984	5,497,422	2,593,322

Wealth Holdings in 1860 (continued)

State: Georgia

County	Male Slaves	Female Slaves	Slave Totals	Land
Borsythe	450,058	374,920	824,978	766,896
Franklin	625,022	571,856	1,196,878	942,449
Fulton	1,449,250	1,267,312	2,716,452	723,345
Gilmer	238,848	60,242	299,090	520,111
Glasscock	400,520	298,288	698,808	345,665
Glynn	991,814	1,202,216	2,194,030	614,582
Gordon	1,066,648	887,448	1,954,096	2,004,875
Greene	4,348,804	3,442,672	7,791,476	1,855,185
Gwinnett	1,242,255	1,051,173	2,293,428	1,116,021
Habersham	364,144	385,440	739,584	725,983
Hall	619,752	543,016	1,162,768	948,172
Hancock	4,418,368	2,870,816	7,289,184	2,179,578
Haralson	120,156	92,288	212,444	314,653
Harris	3,911,394	3,255,624	7,167,018	1,946,175

Wealth Holdings in 1860 (continued)

State: Georgia

County	Male Slaves	Female Slaves	Slave Totals	Land
Hart	700,970	625,087	1,326,057	738,093
Heard	1,455,574	1,156,896	2,612,470	1,143,428
Henry	2,314,584	1,877,896	4,192,480	1,634,542
Houston	5,666,304	434,008	6,100,312	2,524,197
Irwin	122,594	102,881	225,475	143,475
Jackson	1,565,190	1,412,336	2,977,526	1,256,652
Jasper	3,651,056	2,805,720	6,456,776	1,613,478
Jefferson	3,086,112	2,376,416	5,462,528	1,845,175
Johnson	451,112	337,840	788,952	515,880
Jones	3,885,869	2,333,858	6.219,727	1,607,323
Laurens	1,969,926	1,298,624	3,268,550	1,616,319
Lee	2,622,352	1,984,192	4,606,544	2,140,429
Liberty	3,091,382	2,491,776	5,583,158	617,592
Lincoln	1,942,522	1,540,056	3,482,578	782,140

214

Wealth Holdings in 1860 (continued)

State: Georgia

County	Male Slaves	Female Slaves	Slave Totals	Land
Lumpkin	217,124	180,456	397,580	331,295
Macon	2,449,496	2,053,408	4,502,904	1,680,768
Madison	1,012,894	838,008	1,850,902	758,797
Marion	1,858,202	1,429,640	3,287,842	1,140,302
McIntosh	1,935,036	1,587,027	3,522,063	892,061
Meriweather	4,604,926	3,562,976	8,167,902	2,432,794
Miller	304,606	286,752	592,358	314,595
Milton	317,254	253,792	571,046	327,085
Mitchell	787,338	688,854	1,476,202	819,057
Monroe	5,295,296	5,495,488	10,790,784	3,153,690
Montgomery	479,304	381,240	860,544	389,038
Morgan	3,896,638	3,811,264	7,707,902	1,394,573
Murray	611,320	604,816	1,216,136	1,254,805

Wealth Holdings in 1860   (continued)

State: Georgia

County	Male Slaves	Female Slaves	Slave Totals	Land
Muscogee	3,941,960	2,658,224	6,600,184	1,514,052
Newton	3,354,882	2,662,344	6,017,226	1,885,836
Oglethorp	3,614,465	3,043,703	6,658,168	1,766,381
Paulding	288,796	243,904	532,700	671,708
Pickens	119,102	105,472	224,574	384,292
Pierce	113,832	99,704	213,536	208,710
Pike	2,483,224	1,915,800	4,399,024	1,485,948
Polk	1,133,073	992,696	2,125,769	1,331,713
Pulaski	2,189,158	1,635,640	3,824,798	1,485,870
Putnam	3,645,786	2,872,464	6,418,250	1,663,088
Quitman	825,282	679,800	1,505,082	574,730

*   = did not exist in 1850
**   = did not exist in 1860
*** = no record

Wealth Holdings in 1860 (continued)

State: Georgia

County	Male Slaves	Female Slaves	Slave Totals	Land
Rabun	101,184	88,992	190,176	274,926
Randolph	2,216,600	1,883,567	4,100,167	1,443,698
Richmond	4,115,870	3,566,272	7,682,142	2,105,079
Schley	1,177,318	1,003,632	2,180,950	737,130
Scriven	2,368,338	1,832,576	4,200,914	1,444,732
Spalding	1,926,712	1,601,032	3,527,744	989,600
Stewart	4,064,751	3,295,296	7,360,047	2,502,959
Sumter	2,569,652	1,984,192	4,553,844	2,319,466
Talbot	4,527,984	348,224	4,876,208	1,957,372
Taliaferro	1,446,088	1,190,680	2,636,768	661,670
Tatnall	600,780	477,920	1,078,700	305,905
Taylor	1.230,511	910,468	2,140,979	1,078,678
Telfair	407,898	362,560	700,458	295,795
Terrell	1,501,950	1,181,616	2,683,566	1,202,955

Wealth Holdings in 1860   (continued)

State: Georgia

County	Male Slaves	Female Slaves	Slave Totals	Land
Thomas	3,266,346	2,561,816	5,828,162	1,530,540
Towns	51,646	48,616	100,262	260,662
Troup	5,064,127	4,066,789	9,130,916	2,196,064
Twiggs	2,784,668	2,160,528	4,945,196	1,535,777
Union	53,754	52,736	106,490	352,560
Upson	2,548,572	2,002,320	4,550,892	1,413,869
Walker	766,258	859,200	1,625,458	1,469,831
Walton	2,226,708	1,861,992	4,088,700	1,342,409
Ware	238,204	122,776	360,980	381,571
Warren	2,787,830	2,195,136	4,982,966	1,525,824
Washington	3,282,402	2,548,957	5,831,359	2,358,562
Wayne	339,388	240,608	579,996	145,633
Webster	1,187,858	945,128	2,132,986	852,642
White	135,966	110,416	246,382	326,872

218

Wealth Holdings in 1860   (continued)

State: Georgia

County	Male Slaves	Female Slaves	Slave Totals	Land
Whitfield	905,386	706,992	1,612,378	1,546,584
Wilcox	191,600	168,641	360,241	285,977
Wilkes	4,055,792	3,304,240	7,360,032	1,601,158
Wilkinson	2,035,274	1,581,256	3,616,530	1,974,014
Worth	322,524	264,504	587,028	527,872

State: Louisiana

Ascension	4,685,118	3,043,703	7,728,821	6,253,790
Assumption	5,037,288	3,234,362	8,271,590	7,013,350
Avoyelles	4,576,824	2,787,211	7,364,035	5,175,358
Baton Rouge (East)	4,017,024	3,764,957	8,681,981	2,588,300
Baton Rouge (West)	3,121,902	2,257,523	5,379,425	3,650,210
Blenville**				

Wealth Holdings in 1860 (continued)

State: Louisiana

County	Male Slaves	Female Slaves	Slave Totals	Land
Bossier	4,901,916	3,669,474	7.159,439	4,657,057
Caddo	4,167,450	3,313,271	7,480,721	3,843,015
Calcasieu	683,802	510,641	1,194,443	236,920
Caldwell	1,021,734	931,489	1,953,223	1,701,075
Carroll	7,033,464	5,161,251	14,094,715	15,068,712
Catahoula	3,703,403	2,759,411	6,462,814	5,693,255
Clairborne	4,279,716	3,666,094	7,945,810	2,775,080
Concordia	7,194,096	5,434,744	12,628,840	12,335,720
De Soto	4,802,490	3,807,586	8,610,076	2,546,987
Feliciana East	5,707,009	4,867,869	10,664,878	2,218,878
Feliciana West	4,425,607	4,232,658	8,658,265	2,244,516
Franklin	1,867,698	1,580,901	3,448,599	1,674,572
Iberville	6,691,734	4,183,084	10,874,818	12,661,190
Jackson	2,289,546	1,859,350	4,148,896	1,343,760

Wealth Holdings in 1860   (continued)

State: Louisiana

County	Male Slaves	Female Slaves	Slave Totals	Land
Jefferson	3,285,198	1,932,817	5,218,015	2,682,080
LaFayette	1,362,977	2,001,349	4,370,326	1,224,630
LaFourche	3,916,836	2,594,020	6,510,856	4,104,100
Livingston	746,172	585,922	1,332,094	317,038
Madison	7,204,302	5,435,651	12,639,953	11,640,660
Morehouse	3,700,242	2,964,076	6,664,318	5,505,285
Natchitoches	5,625,633	3,811,605	9,437,238	5,059,239
Orleans	6,743,898	7,616,986	14,360,880	1,301,000
Ouichita	1,561,518	1,297,917	2,859,435	2,323,633
Plaquemines	3,282,930	2,178,614	5,461,544	2,791,700
Point Coupee	7,520,688	5,480,094	13,000,782	8,815,520

*   = did not exist in 1850
**   = did not exist in 1860
***   = no record

Wealth Holdings in 1860 (continued)

State: Louisiana

County	Male Slaves	Female Slaves	Slave Totals	Land
Rapides	9,023,789	6,725,836	15,749,625	9,340,611
Sabine	1,003,590	735,577	1,739,167	414,746
St. Bernard	1,524,096	765,508	9,179,604	***
St. Charles	2,684,178	1,587,250	4,271,428	3,261,900
St. Helena	2,148,930	1,629,879	3,778,809	1,460,107
St. James	5,206,072	3,133,956	8,340,028	3,557,050
St. John the Baptist	2,017,782	1,769,557	4,687,339	2,592,800
St. Landry	6,593,076	5,003,012	11,596,088	5,026,118
St. Martin's	4,269,510	3,168,151	7,437,661	4,850,021
St. Mary's	8,133,048	5,256,972	13,390,020	9,737,100
St. Tammany	1,066,386	750,732	1,817,118	168,261
Tensas	8,476,650	6,339,930	14,816,580	15,452,763
Terre Bonne	3,972,402	2,883,353	6,855,755	7,166,390

Wealth Holdings in 1860 (continued)

State: Louisiana

County	Male Slaves	Female Slaves	Slave Totals	Land
Union	2,062,746	1,736,905	3,799,651	1,166,836
Vermillion	735,966	593,178	1,329,144	412,365
Washington	920,992	773,209	1,694,201	247,720
Winn	741,636	625,830	1,367,466	488,190

State: Mississippi

County	Male Slaves	Female Slaves	Slave Totals	Land
Adams	8,637,185	6,840,351	15,477,536	3,000,800
Amite	4,693,960	3,662,406	8,356,456	2,169,575
Attala	2,871,585	2,380,434	5,252,019	2,436,023
Bolivar	5,534,045	4,150,452	9,684,497	8,759,270
Calhoun	1,057,575	869,466	1,927,041	1,260,177
Carroll	8.126,000	6,507,336	14,633,336	8,276,506
Chicksaw	5,475,490	4,187,190	9,662,680	4,509,034
Chocktaw	2,392,390	2,046,024	4,438,414	2,432,510

Wealth Holdings in 1860 (continued)

State: Mississippi

County	Male Slaves	Female Slaves	Slave Totals	Land
Clairborne	7,222,580	5,739,606	12,962,186	4,778,610
Clark	2,957,675	2,407,752	5,365,427	2,293,619
Coahoma	3,227,238	2,347,005	5,574,243	5,100,595
Copiah	4,677,230	3,739,740	8,416,970	1,550,639
Covington	897,445	756,426	1,653,871	428,195
DeSoto	8,325,565	6,553,494	14,879,059	6,578,547
Franklin	2,723,405	2,280,582	5,003,987	1,341,737
Greene	378,815	358,902	737,717	579,110
Hancock**				
Harrison	616,620	459,696	1,076,316	683,900
Hinds	13,333,810	10,373,304	23,707,114	6,240,445
Holmes	7,000,310	5,679,318	12,679,628	6,074,192
Issaquena	4,340,537	3,234,744	7,575,281	6,576,505
Itawamba	2,080,495	1,683,354	3,763,849	2,021,943

Wealth Holdings in 1860   (continued)

State: Mississippi

County	Male Slaves	Female Slaves	Slave Totals	Land
Jackson	702,660	461,580	1,164,240	38,006
Jasper	2,638,560	2,169,426	4,807,986	2,157,167
Jefferson	7,259,625	5,752,794	13,012,419	3,232,595
Jones	234,220	193,110	427,330	351,438
Kemper	3,514,495	2,599,920	6,114,415	2,533,819
LaFayette	4,281,685	3,298,884	7,580,569	3,180,690
Lauderdale	2,987,500	2,401,158	5,388,658	2,032,489
Lawrence	2,178,485	1,748,352	3,926,837	1,286,136
Leake	1,644,676	1,420,888	3,065,564	1,413,378
Lowndes	9,969,885	7,796,934	17,766,819	7,726,605
Madison	10,711,980	8,507,202	19,219,182	8,181,595

*   = did not exist in 1850
**   = did not exist in 1860
***   = no record

Wealth Holdings in 1860   (continued)

State: Mississippi

County	Male Slaves	Female Slaves	Slave Totals	Land
Marion	1,296,575	1,009,824	2,306,399	386,083
Marshall	10,407,255	8,077,650	18,484,905	7,076,960
Monroe	7,609,760	5,907,282	13,517,042	6,446,406
Neshoba	1,300,160	1,045,620	2,345,780	960,192
Newton	1,928,730	1,639,080	3,567,810	1,179,733
Noxubee	9,213,450	7,228,908	16,442,358	8,253,247
Oktibbeha	4,733,395	3,413,808	8.147,203	3,352,455
Panola	5,147,771	3,914,019	9,061,790	3,682,361
Perry	420,640	355,134	775,774	209,598
Pike	2,902,655	2,337,102	5,239,757	1,544,998
Pontotoc	4,515,905	3,565,470	8,081,375	4,264,377
Rankin	4,091,680	3,419,460	7,511,140	3,346,169
Scott	1,806,840	1,339,524	3,146,364	1,528,199
Simpson	1,351,545	1,104,966	2,456,511	879,970

Wealth Holdings in 1860   (continued)

State: Mississippi

County	Male Slaves	Female Slaves	Slave Totals	Land
Smith	,229,655	1,084,242	2,313,897	1,101,771
Sunflower**				
Tallahatchie	3,036,495	2,337,102	5,373,597	3,337,592
Tippah	3,438,440	3,033,650	6,472,090	3,349,432
Tishemingo	3,863,220	3,414,346	5,277,566	2,110,705
Tunica	2,191,630	1,525,098	3,716,728	4,217,575
Warren	9,219,425	5,545,554	14,764,979	5,148,820
Washington**				
Wayne	1,100,595	958,956	2,059,551	347,840
Wilkinson	7,706,555	6,127,710	13,834,265	3,389,407
Winston	2,430,630	2,030,010	4,460,640	1,505,740
Yalobusha	5,541,215	4,246,436	9,787,751	3,235,661
Yazoo	9,968,690	7,773,385	17,742,074	10,287,227

226

Wealth Holdings in 1860   (continued)

State: North Carolina

County	Male Slaves	Female Slaves	Slave Totals	Land
Alamance	1,682,564	1,290,732	2,973,296	1,512,700
Alexander	284,715	243,810	528,515	656,969
Alleghany	95,904	85,140	181,044	482,244
Anson	3,362,634	2,712,096	6,074,730	1,711,978
Ashe	182,817	157,122	339,939	555,503
Beaufort	3,021,975	2,137,788	5,159,763	1,139,020
Bertie	2,981,015	3,119,994	7,101,009	2,061,153
Bladen	2,746,251	1,931,904	4,678,155	2,244,488
Brunswick	1,995,003	1,222,920	3,217,923	755,766
Buncombe	979,020	715,950	1,694,970	1,951,951
Burke	1,208,519	893,206	2,101,725	784,793
Cabarras	1,497,501	1,160,226	2,657,727	1,812,519
Caldwell	482,517	452,790	935,307	879,035
Camden	1,132,866	748,458	1,881,324	1,865,734

Wealth Holdings in 1860   (continued)

State: North Carolina

County	Male Slaves	Female Slaves	Slave Totals	Land
Carteret	972,027	744,588	1,716,615	411,945
Caswell	4,768,227	3,446,622	8,214,849	3,848,743
Catawaba	797,202	657,126	1,454,328	1,715,639
Chatham	3,058,938	2,387,016	5,445,954	2,354,683
Cherokee	242,757	209,754	452,511	1,337,269
Chowan	1,844,154	1,396,296	3,240,450	989,606
Cleveland	1,000,910	839,539	1,840,449	1,310,613
Columbua	1,311,787	942,732	2,154,579	1,081,225
Craven	2,991,006	2,381,598	5,372,604	1,376,387
Cumberland	3,001,995	2,133,918	5,135,913	1,536,839
Currituck	1,353,645	870,750	2,224,395	1,175,485
Davidson	1,460,538	1,203,570	2,664,108	1,988,464
David	1,153,845	925,704	2,079,549	1,388,642
Duplin	3,488,508	2,736,090	6,224,598	3,131,621

Wealth Holdings in 1860   (continued)

State: North Carolina

County	Male Slaves	Female Slaves	Slave Totals	Land
Edgecomb	5,762,832	3,732,338	8,895,060	4,974,920
Forsythe	901,098	650,160	1,551,258	117,800
Franklin	3,483,795	2,732,565	6,216,360	2,453,259
Gaston	1,053,945	849,078	1,903,023	1,529,274
Gates	1,871,127	1,524,006	3,395,133	934,908
Granville	5,423,571	4,250,808	9,674,379	3,457,365
Greene	1,978,020	1,478,340	3,456,360	1,658,998
Guilford	1,773,225	1,402,488	3,175,713	3,406,736
Halifax	5,027,967	3,945,078	8,973,045	3,699,426
Harnet	1,272,726	982,980	2,255,706	992,531
Haywood	153,846	119,970	273,816	730,397

*   = did not exist in 1850
**   = did not exist in 1860
***   = no record

Wealth Holdings in 1860   (continued)

State: North Carolina

County	Male Slaves	Female Slaves	Slave Totals	Land
Henderson	701,298	511,614	1,212,912	1,515,097
Hertford	2,196,140	1,424,326	3,620,466	1,321,818
Hyde	1,476,522	986,076	2,462,509	1,700,075
Iredell	2,082,915	1,583,604	3,666,519	2,292,844
Jackson	133,866	102,168	236,034	616,119
Johnson	2,459,538	1,834,380	4,293,918	1,750,771
Jones	1,705,293	1,268,586	2,973,879	963,266
Lenoir	2,516,481	1,981,440	4,497,921	2,432,030
Lillington	1,611,387	1,299,112	2,910,499	***
Lincoln	1,072,926	785,610	1,858,536	1,380,259
Macon	258,741	195,048	453,789	894,577
Madison	99,996	85,088	185,084	733,397
Martin	2,120,877	1,637,010	3,757,887	1,158,545
McDowell	652,347	492,254	1,144,611	774,416

Wealth Holdings in 1860 (continued)

State: North Carolina

County	Male Slaves	Female Slaves	Slave Totals	Land
Mecklenburg	3,148,848	2,558,844	5,707,692	2,823,949
Montgomery	861,138	722,142	1,582,180	359,341
Moore	1,223,775	980,658	2,294,433	1,178,311
Nash	2,240,757	1,832,058	3,221,414	1,736,608
New Hanover	3,501,495	2,708,226	6,209,721	1,381,687
North Hampton	3,462,534	2,471,382	5,932,916	2,659,031
Onslow	1,643,355	1,388,556	3,031,911	1,337,923
Orange	2,484,003	2,068,086	4,552,089	2,141,690
Pasquotank	1,570,428	1,047,996	2,618,424	1,927,149
Perquimans	1,859,139	1,263,943	3,123,081	15,37,770
Person	2,556,441	1,986,084	4,542,525	1,915,505
Pitt	4,246,749	3,146,310	7,393,059	3,052,010
Polk	287,712	246,132	533,844	435,684
Randolph	782,217	644,742	1,436,959	1,791,483

Wealth Holdings in 1860   (continued)

State: North Carolina

County	Male Slaves	Female Slaves	Slave Totals	Land
Richmond	2,769,228	2,031,750	4,800,978	2,117,985
Robeson	2,722,275	2,067,354	4,789,629	2,355,987
Rockingham	3,048,948	2,479,896	5,528,844	2,628,246
Rowan	1,962,515	1,579,853	3,542,368	2,924,631
Rutherford	1,147,851	934,218	2,082,069	1,100,656
Sampson	3,503,493	2,675,718	6,179,211	3,110,749
Stanly	571,428	448,146	1,019,574	642,061
Stokes	1,197,801	945,828	2,143,629	983,387
Surry	597,402	488,394	1,085,796	1,212,733
Tyrrel	817,182	586,692	1,403,874	455,845
Union	1,096,902	874,620	1,971,522	1,293,504
Wake	5,201,793	4,139,352	9,341,145	3,246,866
Waranga (Watauga)	51,948	38,700	90,648	532,532
Warren	5,149,845	3,927,276	9,077,121	3,338,899

Wealth Holdings in 1860 (continued)

State: North Carolina

County	Male Slaves	Female Slaves	Slave Totals	Land
Washington	1,212,441	948,181	2,160,622	704,919
Wayne	2,707,290	2,062,710	4,770,000	3,012,511
Wilkes	559,440	483,550	1,043,190	1,185,765
Wilson	1,737,261	1,327,410	3,064,671	1,511,672
Yadkin	679,320	564,246	1,243,566	1,106,415
Yancey	154,845	159,444	314,289	944,719

State: South Carolina

County	Male Slaves	Female Slaves	Slave Totals	Land
Abbeville	9,795,861	8,367,606	18,163,457	
Anderson	4,016,396	3,544,840	7,561,236	3,445,350
Barnwell	8,647,530	7,025,520	15,673,050	9,020,033
Beaufort	15,577,284	13,355,706	9,900,652	
Charleston	18,099,996	15,181,860	33,281,856	5,202,502
Chester	5,372,328	4,421,426	9,793,754	4,236,265

Wealth Holdings in 1860   (continued)

State: South Carolina

County	Male Slaves	Female Slaves	Slave Totals	Land
Chesterfield	2,199,135	1,692,075	3,891,210	1,577,209
Clarenon	4,215,828	3,572,660	7,688,488	2,281,227
Colleton	15,393,272	13,414,252	28,807,524	8,818,772
Darlington	5,860,628	4,820,020	10,680,648	4,786,392
Edgefield	12,208,528	9,515,730	21,724,258	8,634,177
Fairfield	7,658,600	6,306,126	13,964,726	6,314,029
Georgetown	9,437,127	7,048,321	16,485,448	5,818,690
Greenville	3,440,716	2,892,814	6,333,330	3,603,522
Horry	1,228,460	911,072	2,139,532	863,735
Kershaw	3,696,688	3,300,230	6,996,918	2,696,232
Lancaster	2,840,364	2,254,422	5,094,786	2,222,478
Laurens	6,761,156	5,204,178	11,965,334	5,810,438
Lexington	3,130,580	2,404,013	5,534,593	3,210,141
Marion	4,802,816	4,082,984	8,885,800	5,351,580

Wealth Holdings in 1860   (continued)

State: South Carolina

County	Male Slaves	Female Slaves	Slave Totals	Land
Marlborough	3,412,960	2,788,554	6,201,514	4,063,766
Newberry	6,925,636	5,475,254	12,400,890	5,423,706
Orangeburgh	8,275,400	6,654,194	14,929,594	5,331,097
Pickens	2,091,980	1,684,200	3,776,180	3,391,505
Richland	5,735,742	4,434,316	10,170,058	2,099,715
Spartanburgh	4,100,692	3,335,578	7,436,210	4,388,642
Sumter	8,314,464	6,652,590	14,967,054	3,893,683
Union	5,445,316	4,293,908	9,739,224	4,747,203
Willismsburgh	5,244,856	4,034,060	9,278,916	2,404,983
York	5,021,780	3,999,574	9,021,354	4,097,393

State: Tennessee

County	Male Slaves	Female Slaves	Slave Totals	Land
Anderson	320,162	250,049	570,211	1,151,340

Wealth Holdings in 1860   (continued)

State: Tennessee

County	Male Slaves	Female Slaves	Slave Totals	Land
Bedford	3,805,424	2,843,160	6,648,584	7,071,904
Benton	281,842	243,600	525,442	974,861
Bledsoe	401,040	284,490	685,530	914,642
Blount	743,038	598,560	1,341,598	3,304,096
Bradley	617,156	530,700	1,147,856	2,559,725
Campbell	201,634	163,560	365,194	748,164
Cannon	549,202	410,640	959,842	2,406,561
Carroll	2,207,948	1,792,200	4,000,148	2,715,288
Carter	194,950	165,300	360,250	1,168,255
Cheatham	1,024,058	827,302	1,851,158	1,587,451
Clairborne	450,056	287,100	737,150	1,558,030

*   = did not exist in 1850
**   = did not exist in 1860
***   = no record

Wealth Holdings in 1860 (continued)

State: Tennessee

County	Male Slaves	Female Slaves	Slave Totals	Land
Cocke	477,906	355,830	833,736	2,320,967
Doffee	825,474	677,730	1,503,204	1,795,893
Cumberland	61,270	54,810	116,080	268,900
Davidson	7,920,540	6,404,860	14,426,400	13,929,974
Decatur	392,128	371,490	763,618	736,009
DeKalb	520,238	481,980	1,002,218	1,858,285
Dickson	1,242,110	920,460	2,162,570	1,541,760
Dyer	1,429,262	1,160,580	2,589,842	2,685,335
Fayette	8,632,439	6,294,990	14,927,429	4,661,335
Fentress	93,576	89,610	183,186	501,776
Franklin	1,945,044	1,534,680	3,479,724	2,772,390
Gibson	3,249,538	2,772,690	6,022,228	6,758,900
Giles	5,809,510	4,824,160	10,633,660	9,099,460
Grainger	573,710	463,710	1,037,420	1,919,203

Wealth Holdings in 1860 (continued)

State: Tennessee

County	Male Slaves	Female Slaves	Slave Totals	Land
Greene	669,514	497,690	1,267,204	5,021,755
Grundy	149,276	110,490	259,766	504,332
Hamilton	777,572	625,530	1,403,102	2,569,445
Hancock	137,022	107,010	244,032	1,090,405
Hardeman	3,984,536	3,376,761	7,361,297	3,173,184
Hardin	846,640	736,890	1,583,530	1,722,067
Hawkins	1,069,440	819,540	1,888,980	2,810,483
Haywood	6,063,502	4,776,300	10,839,802	6,624,331
Henderson	1,723,358	1,499,010	3,222,368	1,798,197
Henry	2,992,204	2,451,660	5,443,864	4,059,828
Hickman	971,408	754,290	1,725,608	1,693,224
Humphreys	807,650	630,750	1,438,400	1,568,223
Jackson	647,234	535,050	1,182,284	1,639,505
Jefferson	1,147,420	916,980	2,064,400	4,224,357

Wealth Holdings in 1860   (continued)

State: Tennessee

County	Male Slaves	Female Slaves	Slave Totals	Land
Johnson	116,473	102,573	219,086	786,806
Knox	1,316,748	1,007460	2,324,208	4,480,870
Lauderdale	1,608,616	1,206,690	2,815,306	1,857,255
Lawrence	624,954	511,560	1,136,574	1,181,148
Lewis	123,654	116,580	240,234	292,050
Lincoln	3,728,558	2,990,190	6,718,748	8,243,905
Macon	536,948	384,540	921,488	1,246,301
McMinn	1,008,170	861,300	1,869,470	2,962,346
McNairy	976,978	875,220	1,852,198	1,865,614
Madison	5,502,046	4,350,000	9,852,046	5,069,307
Marion	344,945	304,690	649,635	1,067,739
Marshall	2,393,986	1,987,950	4,381,936	5,440,318
Maury	7,898,260	6,454,530	14,352,790	15,153,853
Meigs	362,050	269,700	631,750	1,429,660

WEALTH HOLDINGS IN 1860 (continued)

State: <u>Tennessee</u>

<u>County</u>	<u>Male Slaves</u>	<u>Female Slaves</u>	<u>Slave Totals</u>	<u>Land</u>
Monroe	863,350	708.180	1,571,530	3,449,290
Montgomery	5,380,620	4,012,440	9,293,060	6,522,474
Morgan	62,384	54,810	117,194	501,805
Obion	1,308,950	1,049,220	2,358,170	3,479,477
Overton	560,342	501,990	1,062,332	1,653,886
Perry	308,578	234,030	542,608	958,740
Polk	248,122	194,847	389,694	1,076,030
Putnam	350,910	310,590	661,500	889,274
Rhea	344,226	264,480	608,706	1,171,640
Roane	1,015,968	709,920	1,725,888	3,420,610
Robertson	2,671,372	2,101,920	4,773,292	5,211,402
Rutherford	7,072,786	5,655,870	12,728,655	13,468,309
Scott	35,648	23,490	59,138	203,910
Sequatchie	119,198	80,910	200,108	384,780

Wealth Holdings in 1860 (continued)

State: Tennessee

County	Male Slaves	Female Slaves	Slave Totals	Land
Sevier	270,702	249,690	520,392	1,682,698
Shelby	9,159,308	6,935,640	16,094,948	9,428,209
Smith	2,308,251	1,801,087	4,109,338	4,358,147
Stewart	1,528,408	892,620	2,421,028	1,108,369
Sullivan	620,498	440,220	1,060,718	2,792,803
Sumner	4,197,552	3,333,840	7,531,392	6,368,096
Tipton	2,988,862	2,220,240	5,209,102	2,499,118
Union	106,944	72,210	179,154	804,440
Van Buren	137,022	98,310	235,332	392,593
Warren	1,279,986	1,004,850	2,284,836	2,135,840
Washington	504,642	423,690	928,332	4,531,622

* = did not exist in 1850
** = did not exist in 1860
*** = no record

241

Wealth Holdings in 1860 (continued)

State: Tennessee

County	Male Slaves	Female Slaves	Slave Totals	Land
Wayne	714,074	541,140	1,255,214	1,475,887
Weakley	2,220,899	1,989,931	4,210,830	2,942,005
White	597,104	518,520	1,115,624	1,341,198
Williamson	6,722,990	6,401,830	12,124,820	10,528,965
Wilson	4,364,652	3,450,420	7,815,072	9,939,447

State: Texas

County	Male Slaves	Female Slaves	Slave Totals	Land
Anderson	1,941,187	1,717,071	3,658,258	1,764,388
Angelina	389,605	239,046	718,651	469,225
Atacosa	58,150	53,256	111,406	94,126
Austin	2,323,674	1,791,684	4,115,358	3,797,883
Banderah	4,652	7,608	12,260	20,550
Bastrop	1,597,962	1,145,004	2,742,066	1,148,154

Wealth Holdings in 1860   (continued)

State: Texas

County	Male Slaves	Female Slaves	Slave Totals	Land
Bee	47,638	34,236	81,919	142,744
Bell	614,064	1,064,838	1,339,129	
Bexar	773,395	687,573	1,460,968	591,706
Blanco	53,498	49,452	102,950	576,302
Bosque	160,494	147,405	307,899	156,417
Bowie	1,402,616	1,240,583	2,643,199	1,250,661
Brazoria	3,065,668	2,310,930	5,376,598	4,815,608
Brazos	603,597	510,687	1,114,284	1,371,702
Buchanan	17,445	16,167	33,612	3,775
Burleson	1,192,075	9k3,911	2,105,986	1,638,606
Burnet	124,441	120,777	245,218	302,289
Caldwell	924,585	766,406	1,691,091	740,022
Calhoun	207,014	217,779	424,793	44,400
Cameron	2,326	3,804	6,130	854,845

Wealth Holdings in 1860   (continued)

State: Texas

County	Male Slaves	Female Slaves	Slave Totals	Land
Comanche	32,564	31,383	63,947	49,024
Cass	2,345,781	1,881,520	4,227,301	1,209,853
Chambers	291,913	245,358	537,271	275,488
Cherokee	1,824,747	1,571,052	3,395,799	1,261,459
Collin	568,707	525,903	1,094,610	2,090,058
Colorado	2,105,030	1,645,230	3,750,260	3,066,070
Comal	101,181	97,002	198,183	561,527
Cook	203,525	183,543	387,068	548,601
Coryell	167,472	153,111	320,583	506,593
Dallas	593,130	527,805	1,120,935	2,342,875
Denton	134,378	124,026	258,404	532,037
DeWitt	914,118	810,252	1,724,370	1,463,556
Ellis	630,346	528,756	1,159,102	1,050,851
El Paso	8.141	7,608	15,749	103,020

Wealth Holdings in 1860   (continued)

State: Texas

County	Male Slaves	Female Slaves	Slave Totals	Land
Erath	60,476	62,766	123,242	101,809
Falls	1,016,462	793,134	1,809,596	482,563
Fannin	967,616	839,733	1,807,349	1,508,806
Fayette	2,107,356	1,863,009	3,970,365	2,518,614
Fort Bend	2,464,397	1,883,931	4,309,328	3,310,820
Freestone	2,007,338	1,766,958	3,774,206	608,371
Frio	2,326	---	2,326	***
Galveston	842,518	788,817	1,631,335	204,495
Gillespie	19,771	15,216	34,087	164,695
Goliad	427,984	447,921	875,905	448,010
Gonzales	1,863,126	1,481,658	3,344,784	1,377,738
Guadalupe	983,898	848,292	1,832,190	1,149,053
Grayson	747,809	609,591	1,357,400	2,041,180
Grimes	3,288,964	2,485,914	5,774,878	3,043,092

Wealth Holdings in 1860 (continued)

State: Texas

County	Male Slaves	Female Slaves	Slave Totals	Land
Hamilton	12,793	14,265	27,058	6,060
Hardin	102,344	97,953	200,297	65,667
Harris	1,308,431	990,183	2,298,614	478,115
Harrison	5,153,253	4,082,643	9,235,896	2,558,809
Hays	440,777	393,714	834,485	324,567
Henderson	614,064	553,482	1,167,546	498,041
Hidalgo	---	951	951	347,750
Hill	369,834	311,928	681,752	684,253
Hopkins	536,143	503,079	1,039,222	896,977
Houston	1,631,689	1,330,449	2,962,138	1,154,435
Hunt	320,988	281,496	602,484	634,699

*   = did not exist in 1850
**   = did not exist in 1860
***   = no record

Wealth Holdings in 1860   (continued)

State: Texas

County	Male Slaves	Female Slaves	Slave Totals	Land
Jack	20,934	30,432	51,366	23,770
Jackson	673,252	546,652	1,219,904	1,137,864
Jasper	915,281	776,967	1,692,248	732,120
Jefferson	183,754	142,650	326,404	14,955
Johnson	290,750	247,260	538,010	415,848
Karnes	188,406	155,013	343,419	137,132
Kaufman	283,772	271,035	554,807	474,687
Kerr	31,401	46,599	78,000	82,910
Lamar	1,681,698	1,310,478	2,992,176	1,753,350
Lampasa	84,899	75,120	160,028	111,701
Lavaca	1,059,493	750,339	1,809,832	1,328,798
Leon	1,519,084	1,173,643	2,591,727	899,947
Liberty	655,932	476,451	1,132,383	751,645
Limestone	588,478	530,658	1,119,136	663,457

Wealth Holdings in 1860   (continued)

State: Texas

County	Male Slaves	Female Slaves	Slave Totals	Land
Live Oak	53,498	37,089	90,587	97,491
Llano	26,749	29,481	56,230	93,258
McLennan	1,418,860	1,109,817	2,528,677	1,350,268
Madison	377,975	330,948	678,923	272,035
Marion	1,122,295	987,138	2,109,433	359,635
Mason	4,652	13,314	17,966	39,310
Matagorda	1,250,225	962,412	2,212,637	1,414,800
Maveric	---	951	951	***
Medina	61,639	50,403	112,042	165,067
Milam	796,362	696,058	1,492,420	1,142,767
Montague	17,445	19,020	36,465	25,395
Montgomery	1,670,068	1,296,213	2,966,281	543,104
Nacogdoches	1,371,177	1,120,278	2,491,455	1,106,470
Navarro	1,101,361	891,087	1,992,448	1,374,245

Wealth Holdings in 1860   (continued)

State: Texas

County	Male Slaves	Female Slaves	Slave Totals	Land
Newton	590,804	474,549	1,065,353	552,081
Nueces	100,018	119,826	219,844	429,582
Orange	231,437	180,690	412,127	24,598
Palo Pinto	72,106	62,766	134,872	53,095
Panola	1,596,206	1,467,858	3,064,064	1,358,354
Parker	117,463	115,071	232,534	207,456
Polk	2,414,388	1,991,394	4,405,782	2,463,889
Presidio	1,163	2,853	4,016	***
Red River	1,738,685	1,446,471	3,185,156	1,694,258
Refugio	138,397	108,414	246,811	758,651
Robertson	1,332,798	1,049,904	2,382,702	1,616,210
Rusk	3,568,084	2,879,628	6,447,712	2,538,442
Sabine	675,703	532,560	1,208,263	245,347
San Augustin	902,847	822,898	1,725,756	472,062

Wealth Holdings in 1860 (continued)

State: Texas

County	Male Slaves	Female Slaves	Slave Totals	Land
San Patricio	52,335	46,599	98,934	181,193
San Saba	51,172	42,795	93,967	145,807
Shackleford	2,326	6,657	8,983	500
Shelby	843,175	709,446	1,552,621	308,918
Smith	2,812,134	2,407,932	5,220,066	1,843,826
Starr	---	5,706	5,706	117,875
Tarrant	476,830	418,440	895,270	***
Titus	1,395,600	1,164,024	2,559,624	1,448,531
Travis	1,811,954	1,475,001	3,286,955	2,305,038
Trinity	574,215	456,851	1,031,066	281,239
Tyler	666,399	539,217	1,205,616	559,119
Upshur	2,185,277	1,797,390	3,982,667	1,734,452
Uvalde	15,119	13,314	38,433	34,616
Van Zandt	190,732	947,405	338,k37	273,041

Wealth Holdings in 1860 (continued)

State: __Texas__

County	Male Slaves	Female Slaves	Slave Totals	Land
Victoria	826,893	649,994	1,486,887	967,414
Walker	2,445,789	1,921,971	4,267,760	1,525,411
Washington	4,658,978	3,706,998	8,365,976	4,313,993
Webb	2,326	3,804	6,130	854,845
Wharton	1,629,363	1,256,271	2,885,634	1,816,560
Williamson	511,720	427,950	939,670	833,418
Wise	66,291	67,521	133,812	138,870
Wood	555,453	497,184	1,052,637	481,879
Young	56,987	40,893	97,880	27,290
State: __Virginia__				
Accomack	2,553,081	1,705,922	4,259,003	3,979,720
Albemarle	7,189,248	5,201,469	12,390,717	9,157,646

Wealth Holdings in 1860 (continued)

State: Virginia

County	Male Slaves	Female Slaves	Slave Totals	Land
Alexandria	488,796	680,427	1,169,223	853,260
Amelia	3,837,504	2,971.485	6,808,989	2,364,058
Amherst	3,215,124	2,323,161	5,538,285	9,874,596
Appomattox	2,288,132	1,753,137	4,041,269	1,902,558
Augusta	2,852,828	2,128,977	4,981,805	10,997,286
Barbour	41,492	42,282	83,774	2,390,269
Bath	507,012	331,992	839,004	1,455,351
Bedford	5,253,210	3,658,886	8,912,026	6,297,453
Berkeley	766,084	685,908	1,451,992	3,547,566
Boone	67,804	69,687	137,491	579,398

*   = did not exist in 1850
**   = did not exist in 1860
*** = no record

252

Wealth Holdings in 1860 (continued)

State: Virginia

County	Male Slaves	Female Slaves	Slave Totals	Land
Botecourt	1,410,728	1,046,088	2,456,816	3,415,045
Braxton	50,600	42,282	92,882	650,016
Brooke	5,060	8,613	13,673	2,447,903
Brunswick	4,550,964	3,508,623	8,059,587	2,318,267
Buchanan	11,132	14,877	26,009	229,981
Buckingham	4,462,920	3,308,175	7,771,095	3,513,277
Cabell	138,644	131,544	270,188	1,611,815
Calhoun	6,072	1,566	7,638	364,617
Campbell	5,514,201	4,318,907	9,833,108	3,712,579
Caroline	5,105,540	4,268,133	9,373,673	4,407,613
Carrol	119,416	107,271	226,687	867,338
Charles City	1,599,972	1,078,191	2,678,163	1,239,410
Charlotte	4,713,896	3,446,766	2,568,163	1,239,410
Chesterfield	4,441,668	2,991,060	7,432,728	3,263,370

Wealth Holdings in 1860   (continued)

State: <u>Virginia</u>

County	Male Slaves	Female Slaves	Slave Totals	Land
Clarke	1,796,300	1,208,169	3,004,469	3,645,185
Clay	10,120	8.613	18,733	165,344
Craig	213,532	155,817	369,349	943,745
Culpepper	3,278,476	2,527,207	5,805,683	4,985,786
Cumberland	3,503,544	2,442,960	5,946,504	2,355,423
Dinwiddie	6,474,776	4,822,497	11,297,273	2,643,250
Doddridge	10,120	18,009	28.129	1,006,326
Elizabeth City	1,233,628	908,280	2,141,908	1,273,050
Essex	3,332,576	2,588,598	5,921,114	2,439,173
Fairfax	1,498,772	1,319,131	2,717,903	3,866,075
Fauquier	5,128,816	4,035,582	9,164,398	10,062,472
Fayette	131,560	107,271	238,831	1,224,096
Floyd	223,652	194,967	418,619	1,023,165
Fluvanna	2,451,580	1,899,458	4,351,065	2,332,149

Wealth Holdings in 1860   (continued)

State: Virginia

County	Male Slaves	Female Slaves	Slave Totals	Land
Franklin	3,080,528	2,578.128	5,658,656	3,684,634
Frederick	1,099,032	889,488	1,988,520	3,987,045
Giles	394,680	297,540	692,220	1,760,806
Gilmer	25,300	20,358	45,658	622,965
Gloucester	2,181,430	2,230,767	5,049,187	2,001,234
Goochland	3,167,560	2,251,125	5,418,685	2,524,327
Grayson	260,084	217,674	477,758	1,432,258
Greenbrier	780,252	572,373	1,352,625	5,713,422
Greene	985,686	763,425	1,749,111	1,213,979
Greenville	2,142,932	1,576,463	3,719,395	982,900
Halifax	7,549,520	5,628,987	13,178,507	6,922,479
Hampshire	592,020	475,281	1,067,301	3,947,900
Hancock	---	1,566	1,566	1,676,745
Hanover	4,678,476	3,680,883	8,359,359	4,203,120

Wealth Holdings in 1860   (continued)

State: Virginia

County	Male Slaves	Female Slaves	Slave Totals	Land
Haroy	546,480	404,028	950,508	2,579,581
Harrison	259,072	246,645	606,717	4,642,794
Henrico	10,971,092	7,012,548	17,983,640	6,128,610
Henry	2,526,964	1,915,218	4,442,182	2,341,356
Highland	196,328	155,817	352,145	1,535,379
Isle of Wright	1,768,288	1,334,573	1,791,778	1,531,290
Jackson	23,276	23,490	46,766	1,355,201
James City	1,312,564	975,618	2,288,182	1,011,340
Jefferson	2,037,156	1,467,342	3,504,498	5,652,143
Kanawha	1,234,640	732,888	1,967,528	1,895,918
King & Queen	3,059,276	2,367,792	5,427,068	2,454,708
King George	1,800,348	1,436,022	3,236,370	1,933,469
King William	2,685,848	2,184,570	4,870,418	2,568,250
Lancaster	1,418,824	1,111,860	2,530,684	1,307,441

Wealth Holdings in 1860   (continued)

State: Virginia

County	Male Slaves	Female Slaves	Slave Totals	Land
Lee	392,054	336,678	728,732	2,768,031
Lewis	94,116	106,488	200,604	1,327,743
Logan	86,020	48,546	134,566	558,443
Loudon	2,750,616	2,091,393	4,842,009	10,508,211
Louisa	5,258,352	3,770,145	9,028,497	4,461,836
Lunenburg	3,703,902	2,761,641	6,465,561	2,232,979
Madison	2,215,268	1,656,828	3,872,096	2,816,620
Marion	28,336	25,839	54,175	3,115,337
Marshall	14,168	10,962	25,130	2,489,909
Mason	156,860	165,996	322,856	1,951,283
Mathews	1,488,622	1,143,479	2,632,101	1,450,460

*   = did not exist in 1850
**   = did not exist in 1860
*** = no record

Wealth Holdings in 1860   (continued)

State: Virginia

County	Male Slaves	Female Slaves	Slave Totals	Land
Meckleburgh	6,359,408	4,602,474	10,961,882	2,606,956
Mercer	182,160	138,491	320,751	1,540,185
Middlesex	1,181,004	911,412	2,092,416	1,145,060
Monongalia	41,492	45,414	86,906	2,884,916
Monroe	575,828	414,207	990,035	2,768,775
Montgomery	1,138,500	833,895	1,972,395	3,062,680
Morgan	46,552	36,801	83,353	479,987
Nansemond	2,735,436	2,069,469	4,804,905	1,680,210
Nelson	2,174,644	2,330,208	5,504,852	4,009,504
New Kent	1,654,602	1,337,373	2,991,975	1,331,275
Nicholas	81,972	56,376	138,348	3,607,259
Norfolk	4,340,468	3,584,574	7,925,042	2,140,252
North Hampton	1,972,388	1,443,852	3,416,240	2,184,150
Northumberland	1,668,788	1,359,288	3,028,976	1,701,047

Wealth Holdings in 1860 (continued)

State: Virginia

County	Male Slaves	Female Slaves	Slave Totals	Land
Nottoway	3,224,232	2,477,412	5,701,644	1,729,186
Ohio	41,492	43,065	84,557	2,423,520
Orange	2,073,444	2,304,369	5,377,813	3,779,299
Page	396,704	349,218	745,922	2,192,549
Patrick	970,508	844,857	1,815,365	1,278,805
Pendleton	120,428	96,309	216,737	1,606,532
Pittsylvania	7,651,253	5,405,140	13,056,393	5,760,940
Pleasants	6,072	5,481	11,553	649,220
Pocahontas	134,596	90,045	224,641	2,051,780
Powhatan	2,810,324	1,997,433	4,807,757	2,100,284
Preston	31,372	25,839	57,211	2,257,314
Prince Edward	2,845,600	2,662,200	6,507,800	2,957,131
Prince George	2,535,250	1,808,730	4,444,990	1,947,416
Prince William	1,148,620	908,280	2,056,900	2,373,100

Wealth Holdings in 1860 (continued)

State: Virginia

County	Male Slaves	Female Slaves	Slave Totals	Land
Prince Ann	1,623,248	1,179,981	2,803,220	1,860,486
Pulaski	801,504	603,693	1,405,197	2,337,220
Putnam	281,660	237,255	518,915	1,266,492
Raleigh	28,336	22,707	51,043	414,672
Randolph	89,056	73,602	162,658	1,628,295
Rappahannock	1,777,072	1,351,458	3,128,530	2,860,410
Richmond	1,236,664	943,515	2,180,179	1,270,037
Ritchie	13,156	19,575	32,731	1,500,626
Roane	34,408	29,754	64,162	531,702
Roanoke	1,380,368	973,260 1	2,353,637	2,323,226
Rockbridge	438,356	1,431,145	3,559,501	5,785,134
Rockingham	1,133,440	959,958	2,093,398	9,718,613
Russell	594,357	449,574	1,043,931	2,324,483

Wealth Holdings in 1860   (continued)

State: Virginia

County	Male Slaves	Female Slaves	Slave Totals	Land
Scott	251,988	185,571	437,559	2,085,722
Shenandoah	375,452	287,361	662,813	4,035,255
Smythe	551,540	371,925	923,465	2,626,469
South Hampton	2,775,916	1,966,896	4,742,812	1,615,065
Spottsylvania	3,704,932	3,114,774	6,819,706	2,394,424
Stafford	1,634,380	1,266,894	2,901,274	1,536,580
Surry	1,350,008	881,658	2,231,666	1,082,056
Sussex	3,251,556	2,381,103	5,632,659	1,601,905
Taylor	45,540	50,112	95,652	1,090,010
Tazewell	622,513	466,087	1,088,600	2,878,107
Tucker	10,120	7,047	17,167	279,308
Tyler	6,072	8,613	14,685	1,600,003
Upshur	103,224	83,781	187,005	1,665,426
Warwick	565,708	336,690	902,398	406,250

Wealth Holdings in 1860 (continued)

State: Virginia

County	Male Slaves	Female Slaves	Slave Totals	Land
Warren	793,408	596,646	1,390,054	2,205,979
Washington	1,332,804	941,949	2,274,753	4,123,233
Wayne	58,696	64,206	122,902	893,758
Webster	1,012	1,566	2,578	203,722
Westmoreland	1,732,597	1,428,431	3,161,028	1,981,680
Wetzel	3,036	5,481	8,517	1,176,571
Wirt	9,108	10,962	20,070	579,126
Wise	30,360	27,405	57,765	506,618
Wood	85,088	69,687	154,695	1,573,864
Wyoming	35,420	20,358	55,778	234,595
Wythe	1,108,140	817,452	1,925,592	3,793,227
York	1,000,868	700,002	1,700,870	1,167,320

BIBLIOGRAPHY

I. Printed Primary Sources:

DeBow, J.B., ed. Compendium of the Seventh Census. Washington,
    D.C.: A.O.P. Nicholson, 1854.

Finley, Anthony. American Atlas. Philadelphia: By the
    Author, 1826.

Smith, Benjamin E. The Century Atlas of the World. New
    York: The Century Co., 1896.

U.S. Bureau of the Census. Seventh Census, 1850: Preliminary
    Report. Washington, D.C.: 1852.

U.S. Bureau of the Census. Eighth Census, 1860: Preliminary
    Report. Washington, D.C.: 1862.

U.S. Congress. Congressional Directory for the 31st Congress.
    Washington, D.C.: 1850.

U.S. Congress. Congressional Directory for the 35th Congress.
    Washington, D.C.: 1859.

U.S. Congress. Congressional Globe. 27th Congress through
    36th Congress. Washington, D.C.: 1842-1862.

II. Books:

Benson, Lee. Toward the Scientific Study of History.
    Philadelphia: Lippincott, 1868.

Butlin, Noel G. Antebellum Slavery. Canberra: University
    of Australia, 1971.

Bruchey, Stuart W. The Roots of American Economic Growth.
    New York: Harper Torchbooks, 1968.

Bruchey, Stuart W. Cotton and the Growth of the American
    Economy, 1790-1860. New York: Harcourt, Brace &
    World, 1967.

Cairnes, John Elliott. The Slave Power. New York: Harper
     Torchbook, 1969.

Eaton, Clement. The Growth of Southern Civilization, 1790-
     1860. New York: Harper Torchbook, 1963.

Fogel, Robert W. and Engerman, Stanley L. Time on the Cross.
     2 Vols. Boston: Little, Brown, 1973.

Gates, Paul W. Agriculture and the Civil War. New York:
     Alfred A. Knopf, 1965.

Gates, Paul W. The Farmer's Age: Agriculture, 1815-1860.
     New York: Holt, Rinehart & Winston, 1960.

Genovese, Eugene D. The Political Economy of Slavery.
     New York: Pantheon, 1965.

Gray, Lewis C. The History of Agriculture in the Southern
     United States to 1860. 2 Vols. New York: Peter Smith,
     1941.

Hibbard, Benjamin Horace. A History of Public Land Policies.
     Madison and Milwaukee: University of Wisconsin Press,
     1965.

McKay, Robert B. Reapportionment: the Law and Politics of
     Equal Representation. New York: Twentieth Century
     Fund, 1965.

North, Douglass C. The Economic Growth of the United States,
     1790-1860. Englewood Cliffs, New Jersey: Prentice-Hall,
     1961.

Phillips, Ulrich B. American Negro Slavery. Baton Rouge:
     Louisiana State University Press, 1966.

Phillips, Ulrich B. Life and Labor in the Old South. Boston:
     Little, Brown & Co., 1963.

Potter, David M. The South and the Sectional Conflict.
     Baton Rouge: Louisiana State University Press, 1968.

Pressly, Thomas J. Americans Interpret their Civil War.
     Princeton: Princeton University Press, 1954.

Robbins, Roy M. Our Landed Heritage. Princeton: Princeton
     University Press, 1942.

Rohrbough, Malcom. The Land Office Business. New York:
     Oxford Univeristy Press, 1968.

Russell, Robert R. Economic Aspects of Southern Sectionalism, 1840-1861. Urbana: University of Illinois Press, 1924.

Samuelson, Paul. Economics. 8th Ed. New York: McGraw Hill Book Co., 1970.

Silbey, Joel H. The Shrine of Party, Congressional Voting Behavior, 1841-1952. Pittsburgh: University of Pittsburgh Press, 1967.

Silbey, Joel and McSeveney, Samuel, eds. Voters, Parties and Elections. Lexington, Massachusetts: Xerox Publishing Co., 1972.

Stampp, Kenneth M., ed. The Causes of the Civil War. Englewood Cliffs, New Jersey: Prentice-Hall, 1959.

Stephenson, George M. The Political History of the Public Lands from 1840 to 1862. Boston: Richard G. Badger, 1917.

Sydnor, Charles, S. The Development of Southern Sectionalism, 1819-1948. Baton Rough: Louisiana State University Press, 1948.

Sydnor, Charles S. Slavery in Mississippi. New York: Appleton-Century, 1933.

Wellington, Raynor G. The Poltical and Sectional Influence of the Public Lands, 1828-1842. New York: Riverside Press, 1914.

Zahler, Helene Sara. Eastern Workingmen and National Land Policy, 1829-1862. New York: Columbia University Press, 1941.

III. Articles:

Axelrod, Robert. "The Structure of Public Opinion on Policy Issues." Public Opinion Quarterly XXXI (Spring, 1967), 51-60.

Battalio, Raymond C. and Kagel, John. "The Structure of Antebellum Southern Agriculture: South Carolina, A Case Study." Agricultural History, 44 (January, 1970) 25-38.

Benson, Lee. "An Approach to the Scientific Study of Past Public Opinion." Public Opinion Quarterly, XXXI (Winter, 1967-68), 522-567.

Benson, Lee and Strout, Cushing. "Causation and the American Civil War: Two Appraisals." History and Theory, I (1961) 163-85.

Bogue, Alan and Margaret. "Profits and Frontier Land Speculation." Journal of Economic History, XVII (March, 1957) 420-437.

Booner, Thomas N. "Civil War Historians and the Needless War Doctrine." Journal of the History of Ideas, XVII (April, 1956) 193-216.

Bonner, James C. "Profile of a Late AnteBellum Community." American Historical Review, 49 (July, 1944), 663-679.

Boucher, Chancey S. "In Re that Aggressive Slavocracy." Mississippi Valley Historical Review, VIII (June-September, 1921), 13-79.

Celler, Emanuel. "Congressional Apportionment -- Past, Present and Future." Law and Contemporary Problems, 17 (1952), 268-278.

Cole, Arthur. "Cyclical and Sectional Variations in the Sale of Public Lands, 1816-1860." Review of Economics and Statistics, IX (January, 1927), 41-53.

Coles, Harry L. "Some Notes on Slaveownership and Landowner-ship in Louisiana, 1850-1860. Journal of Southern History, IX (1943) 320-327.

Conrad, Alfred, et. al. "Slavery as an Obstacle to Economic Growth in the United States: A Panel Discussion." Journal of Economic History, XXVII (December, 1967), 518-560.

Conrad, Alfred and Meyer, John. "The Economics of Slavery in the Ante-Bellum South." The Reinterpretation of American Economic History ed. by Robert Fogel and Stanley Engerman. New York: Harper & Row, 1971, 342-361.

Dowd, Douglas. "The Economics of Slavery in the Ante Bellum South: A Comment." Journal of Political Economy, LXVI (October, 1958) 440-442.

Dray, William. "Some Causal Accounts of the American Civil War." Daedalus, (Summer, 1962), 578-598.

Durden, Robert F. "J.D.B. DeBow: Convolutions of a Slavery Expansionist." Journal of Southern History, XVII (November, 1951), 441-461.

Engerman, Stanley L. "The Antebellum South: What Probably Was and What Should Have Been." Agricultural History, 44 (January, 1970) 127-142.

Evans, Robert Jr. "The Economics of American Negro Slavery, 1830-1860." Aspects of Labor Economics. Princeton: National Bureau for Economic Research, 1962, 185-243.

Fogel, Robert W. and Engerman, Stanley L. "The Economics of Slavery." The Reinterpretation of American Economic History. New York: Harper & Row, 1971, 311-341.

Foust, James D. and Swan, Dale E. "Productivity of Antebellum Slave Laobr: A Micro Approach." Agricultural History, 44 (January, 1970), 39-62.

Gallman, Robert E. "Self-Sufficiency in the Cotton Economy of the Antebellum South." Agricultural History, 44 (January, 1970), 5-24.

Gates, Paul. Charts of Public Land Sales and Entries." Journal of Economic History, XXIV (March, 1964) 332-338.

Genovese, Eugene D. "Commentary: An Historian's View.: Agricultural History, 44 (January, 1970) 143-148.

Genovese, Eugene D. "Marxian Interpretations of the Slave South." Towards a New Past, ed. by Barton Bernstein. New York: Random House, 1968.

Genovese, Eugene D. "Recent Contributions to the Economic Historiography of the Slave South." Science and Society, XXIV (Winter, 1960), 53-66.

Govan, Thomas P. "Was Plantation Slavery Profitable?" Journal of Southern History, VIII (1942), 513-535.

Parker, William N. "Slavery and Southern Economic Development: An Hypothesis and Some Evidence." Agricultural History, 44 (January 1970), 115-126.

Passell, Peter. "The Impact of Cotton Land Distribution on the Antebellum Economy." Journal of Economic History, XXXI (December, 1971), 917-937.

Passell, Peter and Schmundt, Maria. "Pre-Civil War Land Policy and the Growth of Manufacturing." Explorations in Economic History, 9 (Fall, 1971), 35-48.

Passell, Peter and Wright, Gavin. "The Effect of Pre-Civil War Territorial Expansion on the Price of Slaves," Journal of Political Economy, 80 (November-December, 1972), 1188-1202.

Phillips, Ulrich B. "The Economic Cost of Slaveholding in the Cotton Belt." Political Science Quarterly, 20 (June, 1905), 257-275.

Rainwater, Percy Lee. "Economic Benefits of Secession: Opinions in Mississippi in the 1850s." Journal of Southern History, I (November, 1935), 459-474.

Ramsdell, Charles W. "The Natural Limits of Slavery Expansion." Mississippi Valley Historical Review, 16 (September, 1929), 151, 171.

Rippy, J. Fred. "Mexican Projects of the Confederacy." Southwestern Historical Quarterly (April, 1919), 291-317.

Rose, Louis A. "Capital Losses of Southern Slaveholders Due to Emancipation," Western Economic Journal, 3 (Fall, 1964), 39-51.

Rothstein, Morton. "The Cotton Frontier of the Antebellum South: A Methodological Battleground." Agricultural History, 44 (January, 1970), 149-166.

Saraydar, Edward. "A Note on the Profitability of Antebellum Slavery." Southern Economic Journal, 30 (April, 1964) 325-332.

Shannon, Fred A. "The Homestead Act and the Labor Surplus." American Historical Review, XLI (July, 1936), 637-652.

Sutch, Richard. "The Profitability of Ante-Bellum Slavery -- Revisited." Southern Economic Journal, 31 (April, 1965), 365-377.

Watford, W.H. "Confederate Western Ambitions." Southwestern Historical Quarterly, XLIV (October, 1940), 161-187.

Woodman, Harold. "The Profitability of Slavery: A Historical Perennial." The Journal of Southern History, 29 (August, 1963), 303-325.

Wright, Gavin. "An Econometric Study of Cotton Production and Trade, 1830-1860." The Review of Economics and Statistics, LIII (May, 1971), 111-120.

Wright, Gavin. "New and Old Views on the Economics of Slavery." _Journal of Economic History_, XXXIII (June, 1973), 452-466.

Wolff, Gerald. "The Slavocracy and the Homestead Problem of 1854." _Agricultural History_, 40 (April, 1966), 101-111.

Yasuba, Yasukichi. "The Profitabiltiy and Viability of Plantation Slavery in the United States." _The Reinterpretation of American Economic History_, ed. by Robert Fogel and Stanley Engerman. New York: Harper & Row, 1971, 362-369.

IV.   Unpublished Manuscripts:

Barney, William L. "Road to Revolution: The Social Basis of Secession in Alabama and Mississippi." Unpublished Ph.D. dissertation, Columbia University, 1971.

Hart, Charles R.D. "Congressmen and the Expansion of Slavery into the Territories: A Study in Attitudes, 1846-1861." Unpublished Ph.D. dissertation, University of Washington, 1965.

Passell, Peter. "Essays in the Economics of U.S. Antebellum Land Policy." Unpublished Ph.D. dissertation, Yale University, 1970.

Wright Gavin. "The Economics of Cotton in the Antebellum South." Unpublished Ph.D. dissertation, Yale University, 1969.

Dissertations in American Economic History

An Arno Press Collection

1977 Publications

Ankli, Robert Eugene. **Gross Farm Revenue in Pre-Civil War Illinois.** (Doctoral Dissertation, University of Illinois, 1969). 1977

Asher, Ephraim. **Relative Productivity, Factor-Intensity and Technology in the Manufacturing Sectors of the U.S. and the U.K. During the Nineteenth Century.** (Doctoral Dissertation, University of Rochester, 1969). 1977

Campbell, Carl. **Economic Growth, Capital Gains, and Income Distribution:** 1897-1956. (Doctoral Dissertation, University of California at Berkeley, 1964). 1977

Cederberg, Herbert R. **An Economic Analysis of English Settlement in North America, 1583-1635.** (Doctoral Dissertation, University of California at Berkeley, 1968). 1977

Dente, Leonard A. **Veblen's Theory of Social Change.** (Doctoral Dissertation, New York University, 1974). 1977

Dickey, George Edward. **Money, Prices and Growth;** The American Experience, 1869-1896. (Doctoral Dissertation, Northwestern University, 1968). 1977

Douty, Christopher Morris. **The Economics of Localized Disasters:** The 1906 San Francisco Catastrophe. (Doctoral Dissertation, Stanford University, 1969). 1977

Harper, Ann K. **The Location of the United States Steel Industry, 1879-1919.** (Doctoral Dissertation, Johns Hopkins University, 1976). 1977

Holt, Charles Frank. **The Role of State Government in the Nineteenth-Century American Economy, 1820-1902:** A Quantitative Study. (Doctoral Dissertation, Purdue University, 1970). 1977

Katz, Harold. **The Decline of Competition in the Automobile Industry, 1920-1940.** (Doctoral Dissertation, Columbia University, 1970). 1977

Lee, Susan Previant. **The Westward Movement of the Cotton Economy, 1840-1860:** Perceived Interests and Economic Realities. (Doctoral Dissertation, Columbia University, 1975). 1977

Legler, John Baxter. **Regional Distribution of Federal Receipts and Expenditures in the Nineteenth Century:** A Quantitative Study. (Doctoral Dissertation, Purdue University, 1967). 1977

Lightner, David L. **Labor on the Illinois Central Railroad, 1852-1900:** The Evolution of an Industrial Environment. (Doctoral Dissertation, Cornell University, 1969). 1977

MacMurray, Robert R. **Technological Change in the American Cotton Spinning Industry, 1790 to 1836.** (Doctoral Dissertation, University of Pennsylvania, 1970). 1977

Netschert, Bruce Carlton. **The Mineral Foreign Trade of the United States in the Twentieth Century:** A Study in Mineral Economics. (Doctoral Dissertation, Cornell University, 1949). 1977

Otenasek, Mildred. **Alexander Hamilton's Financial Policies.** (Doctoral Dissertation, Johns Hopkins University, 1939). 1977

Parks, Robert James. **European Origins of the Economic Ideas of Alexander Hamilton.** (M. A. Thesis, Michigan State University, 1963). 1977

Parsons, Burke Adrian. **British Trade Cycles and American Bank Credit:** Some Aspects of Economic Fluctuations in the United States, 1815-1840. (Doctoral Dissertation, University of Texas, 1958). 1977

Primack, Martin L. **Farm Formed Capital in American Agriculture, 1850-1910.** (Doctoral Dissertation, University of North Carolina, 1963). 1977

Pritchett, Bruce Michael. **A Study of Capital Mobilization, The Life Insurance Industry of the Nineteenth Century.** (Doctoral Dissertation, Purdue University, 1970). Revised Edition. 1977

Prosper, Peter A., Jr. **Concentration and the Rate of Change of Wages in the United States, 1950-1962.** (Doctoral Dissertation, Cornell University 1970). 1977

Schachter, Joseph. **Capital Value and Relative Wage Effects of Immigration into the United States, 1870-1930.** (Doctoral Dissertation, City University of New York, 1969). 1977

Schaefer, Donald Fred. **A Quantitative Description and Analysis of the Growth of the Pennsylvania Anthracite Coal Industry, 1820 to 1865.** (Doctoral Dissertation, University of North Carolina, 1967). 1977

Schmitz, Mark. **Economic Analysis of Antebellum Sugar Plantations in Louisiana.** (Doctoral Dissertation, University of North Carolina, 1974). 1977

Sharpless, John Burk, II. **City Growth in the United States, England and Wales, 1820-1861:** The Effects of Location, Size and Economic Structure on Inter-urban Variations in Demographic Growth. (Doctoral Dissertation, University of Michigan, 1975). 1977

Shields, Roger Elwood. **Economic Growth with Price Deflation, 1873-1896.** (Doctoral Dissertation, University of Virginia, 1969). 1977

Stettler, Henry Louis, III. **Growth and Fluctuations in the Ante-Bellum Textile Industry.** (Doctoral Dissertation, Purdue University, 1970). 1977

Sturm, James Lester. **Investing in the United States, 1798-1893:** Upper Wealth-Holders in a Market Economy. (Doctoral Dissertation, University of Wisconsin, 1969). 1977

Tenenbaum, Marcel. **(A Demographic Analysis of Interstate Labor Growth Rate Differentials;** United States, 1890-1900 to 1940-50. (Doctoral Dissertation, Columbia University, 1969). 1977

Thomas, Robert Paul. **An Analysis of the Pattern of Growth of the Automobile Industry: 1895-1929.** (Doctoral Dissertation, Northwestern University, 1965). 1977

Vickery, William Edward. **The Economics of the Negro Migration 1900-1960.** (Doctoral Dissertation, University of Chicago, 1969). 1977

Waters, Joseph Paul. **Technological Acceleration and the Great Depression.** (Doctoral Dissertation, Cornell University, 1971). 1977

Whartenby, Franklee Gilbert. **Land and Labor Productivity in United States Cotton Production, 1800-1840.** (Doctoral Dissertation, University of North Carolina, 1963). 1977

1975 Publications

Adams, Donald R., Jr. **Wage Rates in Philadelphia, 1790-1830.** (Doctoral Dissertation, University of Pennsylvania, 1967). 1975

Aldrich, Terry Mark. **Rates of Return on Investment in Technical Education in the Ante-Bellum American Economy.** (Doctoral Dissertation, The University of Texas at Austin, 1969). 1975

Anderson, Terry Lee. **The Economic Growth of Seventeenth Century New England:** A Measurement of Regional Income. (Doctoral Dissertation, University of Washington, 1972). 1975

Bean, Richard Nelson. **The British Trans-Atlantic Slave Trade, 1650-1775.** (Doctoral Dissertation, University of Washington, 1971). 1975

Brock, Leslie V. **The Currency of the American Colonies, 1700-1764:** A Study in Colonial Finance and Imperial Relations. (Doctoral Dissertation University of Michigan, 1941). 1975

Ellsworth, Lucius F. **Craft to National Industry in the Nineteenth Century:** A Case Study of the Transformation of the New York State Tanning Industry. (Doctoral Dissertation, University of Delaware, 1971). 1975

Fleisig, Heywood W. **Long Term Capital Flows and the Great Depression:** The Role of the United States, 1927-1933. (Doctoral Dissertation, Yale University, 1969). 1975

Foust, James D. **The Yeoman Farmer and Westward Expansion of U.S. Cotton Production.** (Doctoral Dissertation, University of North Carolina at Chapel Hill, 1968). 1975

Golden, James Reed. **Investment Behavior By United States Railroads, 1870-1914.** (Doctoral Thesis, Harvard University, 1971). 1975

Hill, Peter Jensen. **The Economic Impact of Immigration into the United States.** (Doctoral Dissertation, The University of Chicago, 1970). 1975

Klingaman, David C. **Colonial Virginia's Coastwise and Grain Trade.** (Doctoral Dissertation, University of Virginia, 1967). 1975

Lang, Edith Mae. **The Effects of Net Interregional Migration on Agricultural Income Growth:** The United States, 1850-1860. (Doctoral Thesis, The University of Rochester, 1971). 1975

Lindley, Lester G. **The Constitution Faces Technology:** The Relationship of the National Government to the Telegraph, 1866-1884. (Doctoral Thesis, Rice University, 1971). 1975

Lorant, John H[erman]. **The Role of Capital-Improving Innovations in American Manufacturing During the 1920's.** (Doctoral Thesis, Columbia University, 1966). 1975

Mishkin, David Joel. **The American Colonial Wine Industry:** An Economic Interpretation, Volumes I and II. (Doctoral Thesis, University of Illinois, 1966). 1975

Winkler, Donald R. **The Production of Human Capital:** A Study of Minority Achievement. (Doctoral Dissertation, University of California at Berkeley, 1972). 1977

Oates, Mary J. **The Role of the Cotton Textile Industry in the Economic Development of the American Southeast:** 1900-1940. (Doctoral Dissertation, Yale University, 1969). 1975

Passell, Peter. **Essays in the Economics of Nineteenth Century American Land Policy.** (Doctoral Dissertation, Yale University, 1970). 1975

Pope, Clayne L. **The Impact of the Ante-Bellum Tariff on Income Distribution.** (Doctoral Dissertation, The University of Chicago, 1972). 1975

Poulson, Barry Warren. **Value Added in Manufacturing, Mining, and Agriculture in the American Economy From 1809 To 1839.** (Doctoral Dissertation, The Ohio State University, 1965). 1975

Rockoff, Hugh. **The Free Banking Era: A Re-Examination.** (Doctoral Dissertation, The University of Chicago, 1972). 1975

Schumacher, Max George. **The Northern Farmer and His Markets During the Late Colonial Period.** (Doctoral Dissertation, University of California at Berkeley, 1948). 1975

Seagrave, Charles Edwin. **The Southern Negro Agricultural Worker:** 1850-1870. (Doctoral Dissertation, Stanford University, 1971). 1975

Solmon, Lewis C. **Capital Formation by Expenditures on Formal Education, 1880 and 1890.** (Doctoral Dissertation, The University of Chicago, 1968). 1975

Swan, Dale Evans. **The Structure and Profitability of the Antebellum Rice Industry:** 1859. (Doctoral Dissertation, University of North Carolina at Chapel Hill, 1972). 1975

Sylla, Richard Eugene. **The American Capital Market, 1846-1914:** A Study of the Effects of Public Policy on Economic Development. (Doctoral Thesis, Harvard University, 1968). 1975

Uselding, Paul John. **Studies in the Technological Development of the American Economy During the First Half of the Nineteenth Century.** (Doctoral Dissertation, Northwestern University, 1970). 1975

Walsh, William D[avid]. **The Diffusion of Technological Change in the Pennsylvania Pig Iron Industry, 1850-1870.** (Doctoral Dissertation, Yale University, 1967). 1975

Weiss, Thomas Joseph. **The Service Sector in the United States, 1839 Through 1899.** (Doctoral Thesis, University of North Carolina at Chapel Hill, 1967). 1975

Zevin, Robert Brooke. **The Growth of Manufacturing in Early Nineteenth Century New England.** 1975